Yesterday's
FLORIDA KEYS

Yesterday's FLORIDA KEYS

by Stan Windhorn and Wright Langley

K&
YP
THE KETCH & YAWL PRESS
MARATHON, FLORIDA

Copyright ©1974 by Stan Windhorn & Wright Langley

Library of Congress Catalog Card Number 74-76691

ISBN-10: 0-9788949-6-0
ISBN-13: 978-0-9788949-6-2
(Previous ISBN: 0-911607-00-5)

Manufactured in the United States of America

Sixteenth Printing, 2008.

The Ketch & Yawl Press, LLC
2315 Overseas Highway, Marathon, FL 33050
or PO Box 5828, Lakeland FL, 33807

Contents

Foreword

WHEN JOHN LEE WILLIAMS traveled the Florida Keys in the early 1830s making observations incorporated into his book, "The Territory of Florida," he wrote, "The Florida Keys are altogether an extraordinary archipelago of islands and reefs."

Williams never intended his book, published in 1837, to be a literal, historical account, and his information is often incorrect. In his assessment of the island chain, however, he is correct. With the world's coastlines mapped, geographers know there is, in character and composition, no other archipelago on this planet to duplicate the Keys.

Their history, like their physical character, similarly defies comparison to other geographic locations on earth. And, like Williams, the authors do not intend this as a literal history. Whatever previously unpublished information this book contains was drawn from memories and photographs of Keys pioneers, their children and their children's children. Memory is intended to reflect a single individual's past experiences, aspirations and emotions. It is seldom a totally accurate recorder.

Even more emphatically, this is no scholarly offering in which the reader is burdened with extraneous information as to precise populations, land acreages, definition of flora and fauna, or a chronology of settlers. In 461 years, various Keys have been given many different names and our intent is to limit use to those most familiar to the reader.

This is, we hope, a simple and brief prose story accompanied by photographs which will provide a visual answer to the question most frequently asked by those residents and visitors who have, in tremendously increasing numbers, come to these Keys in the migrations following 1950. Their question is: "What did it used to be like?"

This attempted reply materialized through the kindness and cooperation of many residents, both old and new, who love these palm fringed bits of coral, limestone, and oolite—tiny fragments of precious stone laid into a background of sky and water that can be believed only by those who have seen them.

Following each caption, we have identified our source since some visual material is a copy of a copy and the original source is unknown. If the photographer or artist is known, the name follows the source. Material not attributed is usually from the authors' collection. We felt this procedure would be helpful to others who delve into the history of the Keys.

For their help and shared affection, our thanks to:

Charles H. Anderson, to whom we are especially indebted for the many photographs from his historical collection and for his printing of many others, and to Shirley Faye Albury, Joe Allen, Benjamin E. Archer, Ida Barron, Mrs. Gloriana Bayly, Sam Boldrick, Jeff Broadhead, Betty Bruce, Mr. and Mrs. Homer Byrum, Bob and Nancy Cain, Carlton J. Corliss, Radford Crane, Mr. and Mrs. John A. Curry, Frank Fontis, County Mayor Harry Harris, Al Key, Mrs. Jack C. Key Jr., Capt. Steve Klem, Mr. and Mrs. Neil M. Knowles, Mayor Del Layton, Margaret Leibel, Mrs. Bud Ley, Bruce Lind, Capt. and Mrs. Eugene Lowe, Elizabeth McIver, Arthur McKee Jr., Mrs. H.S. McKenzie, Ray Matcovich, Mrs. Allen Morris, Dr. Richard Mudd, Mrs. Pauline Papy, Mr. and Mrs. Alton Park, Arva M. Parks, Mr. and Mrs. William A. Parrish Jr., Al Perez, LeBaron Perrine, Dr. Thelma Peters, Peter Pierce Jr., Florence Rabon, Vivienne Roberts, Betty Rondeau, Arthur Rothstein, Mrs. O. A. Sandquist, Judge and Mrs. Lew Schlegel, Mr. and Mrs. Harry Snow Sr., Maud Spence, Alexander (Sandy) Sprunt IV, Mrs. George Stricker Sr., Eddie and Etta Parker Sweeting, Jack Watson, Louise White, George Wielander, Jack and Kay Wilkinson and to our wives, Joan Langley and Jan Windhorn.

Our thanks go to these libraries, agencies, museums, and businesses who made photographs available:

Monroe County Public Library (MCPL); Miami Dade Public Library (MDPL); Monroe County Commission (MCC); Florida State University Strozier Library (FSU); Library of Congress (LC); Historical Association of Southern Florida (HASF); Monroe County Mosquito Control District (MCMCD); U.S. Fish and Wildlife Service; Charley Toppino and Sons, Inc.; U.S. Navy and Navy Aqueduct; Key West Pirate and Torture Museum; Florida Division of Archives, History and Records Management; and Treasure Salvors, Inc.

Key West, Florida

Stan Windhorn
Wright Langley

Yesterday's Florida Keys

THE SPANIARDS called them *Los Martires* when they viewed the Florida Keys from distances safely beyond the coral reefs which were to bring disaster to many a ship and death to many a sailor.

From those deeper and safer turquoise waters of the Gulf Stream the appellation of "the martyrs" came from their tangled, twisting appearance—shapes suggesting suffering.

Suffering these islands and their people have known. It has ranged from that experienced by earliest Indian tribes who lost their isles of plenty to increasingly greater forces of redmen pressing ever southward, to that known by white men and women who came to be plagued by innundating swarms of mosquitos and sandflies and then to have their homes, their loved ones and often themselves destroyed by hurricanes.

The land areas, known as *cayos* (small islands) to the Spanish, *Keys* to the English, found an anguish of their own in unrestrained ravaging of their hardwood forests, their wildlife, their birds, by both man and a violent nature and, finally, by slower more subtle ecological change first noted in mid-century as post-World War II newcomers began a gradual assault on fragile islands ill designed by nature to accommodate population pressures.

Los Martires—members of Ponce de Leon's 1513 expedition first applied that name when this conquistador received possibly undeserved credit for discovery of Florida.

Substantial history indicates that Sebastian Cabot discovered Florida and, at least, the most northern of her loosely defined Keys in 1498. It is equally possible that Columbus saw the southernmost Keys in his 1492 voyage of discovery. Sailing from the Bahamas in search of Cuba, Columbus made reference to small islands, inaccessible to sailors because of reefs and shallow water, seen to the north.

It is even more probable that unknown slavers were the first to come to the

9

THE FLORIDA KEYS are called "Martyres" in this 1564 map drawn by Frenchman Jacques le Moyne. Spaniards named them "Los Martires" supposedly because of the twisted shapes of the Keys. Both spellings were frequently used on early maps. Cartographers of this period clumped the Keys together under the mainland of Florida. (LC)

Keys. Enslaved Indians from Florida were in Cuba, Puerto Rico, and Dominica before Ponce de Leon organized his 1513 voyage.

The age of the Keys is as debatable as that of a fading movie queen. Historians say they are 50,000 years old, but many geologists feel they could be 100,000 years older. Disparity in estimates stems from the fact that the Keys were slow in emerging from their coral, limestone, and oolite foundation, with emergence coming at different times. Geologists suggest that most of the Keys have been above and below water four times since the Pleistocene Era.

More important than who the earliest visitors were is what they saw. Ponce de Leon, sailing down the Florida coast from the St. John's River to the Keys, saw islands heavily forested with trees common to the Caribbean, and other islands which would have been tidal flats except for their solid carpeting of soil-building red mangroves. In a dense tangle of jungle comprising the interior of the Keys were found panther, bear, and deer.

Along beaches were Indians described by some of Ponce's crew as seven feet tall—undoubtedly an exaggeration. They were of the Calusa nation, separated by the Everglades from others of their tribe who controlled much of the Florida West Coast south from Tampa Bay. They were non-agricultural and their social organization was not highly developed. They lived in ease on readily obtainable shellfish.

Unless blinded by lust for gold, the single spectacle which first impressed the conquistador was that of the sky and the sea, bluer than the Mediterranean they knew well, and the overwhelming vision within which this 200-mile chain of islands are the merest punctuation marks.

This was the panorama seen by Ponce de Leon, this remains the panorama of the Keys today. Their character changed imperceptibly during the 250 years in which Spain owned them. In 1763, they came under British rule and it was then that creeping change began. What took place lies in accounts of how the Keys are in the mid-twentieth century and what has happened since the first woodcutters, turtlers, and fishermen came from the Bahamas in increasing numbers after 1763.

Beginning on Elliott, arbitrarily chosen as our northernmost Key, in 1950 there was little that suggested change to the sailor cruising east from the mainland mooring at Homestead's Bayfront Park. The beaches remained attractive, and behind them were the coconut palms, the successors to those trees felled by extremely severe hurricanes of the 1920s.

Eight miles long and no more than a mile wide, it is impossible to press far inland on Elliott Key before the explorer approaches its Atlantic beaches, locations where in Prohibition years smugglers unloaded thousands of gallons of illicit liquor brought from the Bahamas. Elliott and Old Rhodes, the Key immediately to the south, were favored transshipment points, not

HURRICANES tossed treasure-laden Spanish galleons and merchant ships acrosss the jagged coral reef off the Florida Keys. In 1622, a fleet of 28 ships left Havana bound for Spain, but they ran into a tropical storm and five were sunk, including the galleons *Nuestra Senora de Atocha* and *La Margarita*. (Archives of Seville).

only for liquor but for an occasional boatload of Orientals brought from Cuba. In some measure, all of the Keys were put to similar misuse.

But mostly, over the years, these islands have seen fishermen and sponge gatherers. Neither key has sustained a community, as such, but at various times as many as 30 to 40 people have farmed on Elliott. Chief success has come to those who planted pineapple fields and key lime groves. For a time in the 1930s, Charles M. Brookfield, Florida representative of the National Audubon Society, operated Ledbury Lodge there as a sports fishing camp.

Russell and Charlotte Niedhauk lived there in the depression years of the 1930s. Mrs. Niedhauk recalls living off the land and sea at a cost of well below $5 a week. Then and now a few owners have kept weekend homes on the islands.

In 1950 the Niedhauks were 60 miles on down the Keys, still occupying an island approachable only by water, and then open to only a limited few. They supervise Lignumvitae Key, just west of the Matecumbes, and are its sole residents. Purchased by Nature Conservancy Inc., and given to the State of Florida, the preserved Key is named for a native tree with wood so heavy it sinks in water.

Passing Old Rhodes Key, a haven for fisherman and weekenders, the sailor crosses Rhodes Channel and, simultaneously, from Dade to Monroe County. Ahead is Angelfish Creek and North Key Largo. Here is a beginning of the Ocean Reef Club, first evidence of a planned community. Here, too, by 1950

12

was a sight seen frequently along the Keys—level, treeless appendages of shell and crushed limestone bleached white by a near tropical sun.

These were new waterfront building sites dredged from shallow bay bottoms or created with fill accrued in digging 30-foot deep canals to serve future homeowners. The voracious maw of the dragline is a boon to the developer and the bane of the conservationist. One sees it as creating homesites, and profit, from tidal flats, the other as destroyer of vital mangroves and nutrient marine vegetation. In mid-century, the Florida legislature was still more than a decade removed from passage of laws to control land and bay bottom use.

Leaving Ocean Reef and the nearby Anglers Club, the jungle that has always been North Key Largo begins. State Road 905 is a narrow passage through the tangled adult mangrove pressing in from either side.

It is in this area that pirate lore of the Keys centers. Those who mingle legend with fact have every brigand from Sir Francis Drake to Ma Barker burying treasure in the Keys, but mentioned most often as "the Keys' Pirate" is Black Caesar. He is reported to have headquartered on Elliott Key and Key Largo. Storytellers have him keeping a harem of beautiful captives on Old Rhodes.

Only recorded attention given him is that a pirate called Black Caesar was a member of the buccaneering crew of Edward Teach, alias Blackbeard. After Blackbeard was killed in combat with the crew of a British man-of-war, the captured Caesar was taken to Williamsburg, Va., where he was hanged in 1718.

Farther down State Road 905, near a point where it meets U.S. Highway 1, now the 42-bridge lifeline for the Keys it joins, the 1950s traveler would have met John A. Curry depositing children of the Carey families at acreage cleared for homes and truck farming. They came all the way from the Tavernier School which offered grades one through 11.

EDWARD TEACH, better known as Blackbeard, "the fiercest pirate of them all," ranged the Atlantic Coast down into the Caribbean. Pirate legends abound on the Keys. Caesar's Creek, north of Key Largo, is supposedly named after Black Caesar, a trusted member of Blackbeard's crew. (Key West Pirate and Torture Museum)

JOHN JAMES AUDUBON, the renowned bird painter, visited the Florida Keys in 1832. He stopped at Indian Key, Key Vaca (Marathon), Key West, and Dry Tortugas. Fine reproductions of his paintings—some from this expedition—are on display at the Audubon House in Key West.

Down at the fork dividing 905 from U.S. 1, Curry would explain that while newcomers tended to call the entire 27-mile length of the island Key Largo, natives used the name only to identify an area just south of this point, a point where the two-lane main highway veers northwest to leave the Keys at Jewfish Creek. The area designated by Curry as Key Largo is where the depot stood during the 27 years Henry Flagler's Florida East Coast Railroad passed this way.

Off in the Atlantic, to the east of where the depot stood, is the nation's largest reef of living coral which became John Pennekamp Coral Reef State Park, the only underwater park in the hemisphere. It was named for John Pennekamp, associate editor of *The Miami Herald,* who in 1950 answered to the title, "Mr. Conservation."

Curry told his visitor that he lived three miles farther south, past Newport, and in the section known as Rock Harbor. He farmed when he wasn't driving a school bus, and raised three crops a year of tomatoes and melons. Curry's speech vaguely, and correctly, suggests origin in England. His is the speech of those native to the Keys most of whom came from the Bahamas. Some are descendants of loyalists who fled the Carolinas and Georgia during the American revolution and settled on crown soil. Many others are descendants of members of the Eleutherian Society who left England in 1649-50 to seek religious freedom in the Bahamas.

THE EARLIEST WRECKERS of the Keys were probably Calusa Indians. Late in the eighteenth century men came over from the Bahamas for wood-cutting and turtling in the Upper Keys. They noticed the number of wrecks and returned to make a living by wrecking. (MCPL)

INDIAN KEY is an eleven-acre island located just off the Lower Matecumbe. Indians used the Keys as a stopping off point in their journeys, and in 1825 a wrecker, Capt. Jacob Housman bought out the squatters living on the Key. Dissatisfied with the Key West wrecking court, Housman established his own kingdom on Indian Key and through political maneuvering had it designated the county seat of Dade County. (*Harper's New Monthly*)

Devoutly religious (Methodist), honest and possessed of great family pride, these settlers and their progeny are still called Conchs (pronounced Konks). The name derives from their liking for broths, chowders, and fritters made from the muscle of the Queen Conch shell. Old-timers came to farm, to grow pineapples, tomatoes, melons, and key limes. Those who came much earlier were seafarers and fishermen, Bahamian transients who stayed long enough to cut mahogany to build their boats before returning to those islands. The early farmers cut the hardwoods to clear their land. Believing the supply of fine wood limitless, as it then seemed, they simply burned cut timber and used the ash for fertilizer.

Permanent settlement came slowly to Key Largo, but after dawn of this century there were the Careys on North Largo, Pinders in Newport, the Bethels were arriving in Rock Harbor with the Currys soon to come, and south to Mandalay were the Alburys, Russells, Feltons, Sassers, and Sawyers.

In his book, "The Florida Keys and the Coral Reef," Oliver Griswold reports of this period, "In scattered settlements on the Keys, Conch life was rustic, simple, picturesque—partly maritime, partly farming." Lest this create a wrong impression, Griswold adds hastily, "But no one ever called it idyllic. The sandflies, horseflies, doctorflies, and mosquitoes bit saint and sinner alike."

We have met John Curry and now we meet his wife, Elizabeth, as she recalls early life on Largo. Her parents, J. Bunion and Ma Lily Bethel, came to Key West from the Bahamas in 1896, and then to Rock Harbor. "There were times when there were mosquitoes so thick they'd blacken the side of a house," Mrs. Curry remembers. "Had to keep smudge pots burning outside and people's eyes were always red and inflamed." Cheesecloth was used for window screening and to provide bed netting.

A POST OFFICE was established at Indian Key in 1834. Housman built the Tropical Hotel for visitors. The swanky place attracted such a crowd that Audubon complained the boisterous square dancing by villagers distracted him from his sketching. (*Pensacola Gazette*, June 14, 1834)

New Post Office.

A POST OFFICE has been established at Indian Key, Florida. All letters and papers for persons residing on this Island, at Cape Florida, Kayo-Biscayno, New River, Key Vacas, on board the light ship Florida, or on board any of the wrecking vessels, excepting the Pizarro, will reach their intended destination most readily if mailed for this Office.

H. S. WATERHOUSE, P. M.
Indian Key, (Florida,) May, 15, 1834.

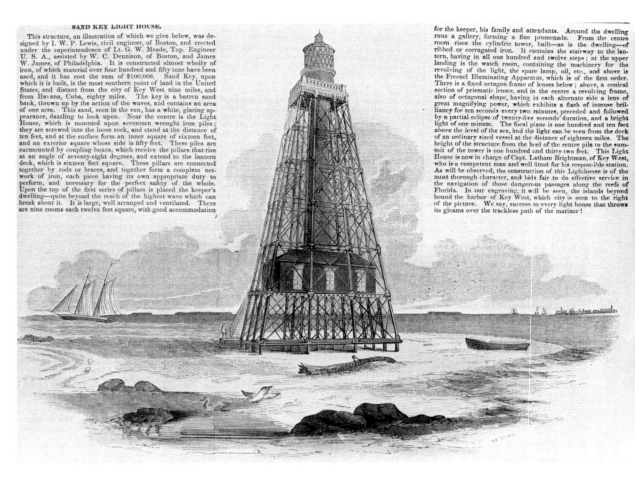

INCREASED SHIPPING along the Florida coastline prompted the United States Government to begin a series of permanent lighthouses along the reef in the early 1850s. Sand Key Lighthouse, some seven miles south of Key West was completed in 1853. The light is 110 feet above sea level and can be seen some 18 miles away. (MCPL)

Until construction of the Navy pipeline from mainland wellfields in 1941, most fresh water was collected in cisterns. The nearest doctors were in Homestead or Key West. Until post World War II expansion of the Florida Keys Electric Cooperative, formed in 1941, kerosene lamps provided lighting. Cooking was usually done in a detached building over buttonwood fires built in a wood range. And, for women, all this was done in ankle length dresses and long-sleeved shirtwaists. The story of the early Key Largo settler can be repeated by all Keys pioneers living outside Key West.

Moving the length of Key Largo, the 1950 traveler would have found those names his father noted 40 and 50 years earlier. The surge of population was still to come so permanent settlers were few, however in many instances sons and grandsons had turned from farming to more profitable work. Florida Keys fishing had gained an international renown, so many began guiding the wealthy and near-wealthy who, in mid-century, represented the bulk of

CONCHS, descendants of Americans who were granted land in the Bahamas, settled in the Upper Keys to farm and fish, and built the typical cabins on the Keys as depicted by *Harper's New Weekly* in 1871.

winter visitors. There were two or three resorts, scattered tourist accommodations, four restaurants, and three bars, periodically lined wall to wall with slot machines. And during prohibition years nearly every key had its favorite bootlegger to meet the wants of the visitor. Offspring of the early farmers were operating some of these businesses, others were in building trades to meet the increasing demand for homes, two turned to selling real estate, and one who operated a nursery would landscape the homes being built for new arrivals.

At the south tip of Key Largo, by 1950, Tavernier was home to approximately 250 permanent residents whose predecessors bore the names Lowe, Albury, Pinder, Johnson, Riley and Smith.

As early as 1875 Tavernier and surrounding islands, including offshore Rodriguez Key, Julia Key, and Planter, would be producing up to one million crates of pineapples a year along with key limes, tomatoes, and melons. Captain Ben Baker settled what is now Planter and grew pineapples about 1866. Sam and Caroline Johnson came 20 years later to farm at Planter and give it its name. In 1882, Amos and Eliza B. Lowe came to homestead a grant of 146 acres encompassing the south one-third of Tavernier. The land stretched from the Atlantic to Florida Bay.

By 1950, several previously occupied offshore islands near Tavernier showed no sign of human use except for the stacked crawfish traps commercial fishermen might keep on them. On one of the islands, Bottlepoint Key, six miles into Florida Bay from Tavernier, was located one of the few Florida breeding areas for the distinctive and colorful roseate spoonbill. In the spring of 1940, when the breeding colony was discovered, Robert Porter Allen, director of sanctuaries for the National Audubon Society, came to the island to live while studying the birds. The colony has increased and thrived and today national research headquarters for the society is a few miles to the south on Plantation Key.

Businesses lining U.S. 1 were much in evidence in 1950 with homes obscured by trees and foliage that drop down to Florida Bay and eastward toward the Atlantic. Most noticeable of businesses were the collection of "Tavern Stores," service station, garage, restaurant, gift shop and former theater building. The enterprises were owned by a 1928 arrival, H. S. McKenzie.

Although the 3,500 mid-century residents of those Keys lying outside Key West did not represent a substantial block of voters, Harry Harris, operator of a Tavernier bar and restaurant, had recently become one of the first Upper Keys men elected to county office. As county commissioner, he was destined to serve more than a quarter-century.

Much in evidence, too, was the generating plant and main offices of the REA-affiliated electric cooperative, spearheaded to creation by Eugene Lowe, grandson of the community's first homesteader and now a charterboat

18

GREEN TURTLES were once plentiful in the waters of the Keys. Turtles that came ashore to lay eggs were "turned" or flipped over on their backs. Unable to right themselves, the turtles remained until later collected. Settlers kept live turtles in water pens, or crawls, until they were butchered for food. (Harper's *New Weekly*)

captain. Organized in 1941, Lowe recalls it appeared impossible to get necessary generating equipment and power lines to begin electrical service during World War II. Fortunately, one of the many notables who came to fish with Captain Lowe was Charles E. Wilson, vice-president of General Electric and then drafted into government service to head the War Production Board. "Mr. Wilson came for a short vacation during the war and while we were fishing I mentioned how we had the Coast Guard here and a research program carried on by Massachusetts Institute of Technology, and how badly we needed electricity," the skipper recalls. "He just smiled and nodded his head, but two weeks later we had everything we needed to start the co-op."

Toward the bay and behind the business houses was the Upper Keys public school, presided over by Charles C. Albury. The "professor", who began teaching down on Pigeon Key and in Marathon in the early 1930s, dedicated most of his life to education and was soon to become principal of the Upper Keys first high school, Coral Shores, planned by 1950 but three years from reality.

Also living here was Mrs. J. Roy (Frances) Tracy, who "retired" to the keys in 1937 only to spend the next 14 years working longer hours than she had ever known. A registered nurse, Mrs. Tracy was on twenty-four hour call treating the ill and injured. Dr. Harvey Cohn did not come until 1953 to open a clinic and relieve her of her freely given services which earned for her the title, "Angel of the Keys."

Below Tavernier is Plantation Key, sparsely settled and long home to truck farmers and fishermen. Here, in 1885, John (Johnny Brush) Pinder built the

Island Home, best known of the Keys' trading schooners. Sizeable parcels of cleared land were purchased on Plantation in 1950, and in isolated places along Florida Bay draglines were at work with their suggestion of an early population influx. Near the lower end of the island was a newly completed fortress-like building whose interior housed coins and treasures still not appraised.

This is Arthur McKee's Sunken Treasure Museum. McKee, a hard-hat diver from Philadelphia and Baltimore, came to the Keys in the 1940s and located wreckage of three Spanish galleons included in the treasure fleet of 1733. There were 21 ships in the fleet, and 17 broke up on reefs along the Keys during a July hurricane. Although most of their $12 million in gold and silver was salvaged by Spaniards the following year, much treasure still remained. Later McKee worked many other finds. A large portion of what he recovered went on display in his museum.

Beyond the museum is Windley Key where the visitor would see a limestone quarry which is worked spasmodically for building stone. Bernard Baruch, financier and adviser to presidents, was once one of its owners. New on tiny Windley, once aptly named Umbrella Key, was the Theater of the Sea, a display of marine life with an always popular dolphin show.

Across Whale Harbor bridge is Upper Matecumbe Key, four miles of narrow island rapidly filling with business places, new and expensive homes, and plush resorts. Upper Matecumbe and Islamorada are one and the same, the latter name having been given the Key by Mary and Nora, daughters of William Krome who became chief construction engineer for Flagler's railroad when it bridged the Keys. In Spanish, Islamorada means isles of purple, and this is the color suggested when the island is viewed from the Atlantic. And, in noting the Atlantic, the visitor may puzzle over its calm water, the absence of surf. Here, and throughout the Keys, normal ocean breakers dissipate on reefs which extend two to 12 miles off-shore. The inshore shallows are normally as placid as a rustic pond.

A three-way division of Islamorada brought the island its first permanent settlers. Richard H. and Mary Ann Roberts Russell who moved the 40 miles from Key Vaca to homestead the north one-third of the Key came in 1882. When the disasterous hurricane struck on Labor Day in 1935 the Russells had grown to a family numbering 77, and when survivors were counted, only 11 remained.

In 1883 Richard and Caroline Pinder came from the Bahamas via Key West, then Florida's largest city, to claim the middle third of the island. One of their sons, Preston Pinder, became first of the fishing guides in 1902. Finally, William and Edna Parker came from Key West to take title to the south one-third of the Key. Like the Russells, the Pinders and Parkers were prolific, but the Parkers, unlike others, were the only family to remain intact through the 1935 disaster. One group of 13 family members stood against the flooding waters on an old double iron bed in a second-floor bedroom to escape alive.

Two of those who stood on the bed through the hurricane, which sent barometers to 26.35 inches, the lowest reading ever recorded in this hemisphere, were newly married Eddie and Etta Parker Sweeting. When the estimated 200 to 250-miles-an-hour winds subsided, no building in Islamorada was undamaged and few were standing and recognizable. Eddie Sweeting, a contractor and store-keeper, was first to build a new structure on the island, a two-story grocery with a second-floor apartment. The total death toll recorded in an area stretching from Long Key to Tavernier was 423, and with them died the Overseas Railroad.

Henry Flagler was dead, his railroad was in bankruptcy, and the nation was in the depths of a depression. Directors decided against making repairs to tracks and bridges, and sold the right of way to the county's toll bridge commission.

Between Upper and Lower Matecumbe are four bridges, two causeways and tiny Tea Table Key. To the west is Lignumvitae Key, home of the Niedhauks whom we found earlier on Elliott Key. To the east in the Atlantic is Indian Key, once known as Matanzas because of the reputed killing by Indians there of 400 Frenchmen. Whether the Frenchmen were slaughtered—or if they ever existed—is doubtful; however, the island is not without its bloody history.

Those seafaring salvagers known as the wreckers played an early and prominent role in Florida Keys history. Atlernately proclaimed saints or sinners, they grew wealthy competing for salvage rights to vessels broken up on the unlighted reefs of the Keys. Key West became their headquarters soon after it was established in 1822, and a federal court was created there to rule on salvage claims. From Key West, wreckers ranged the length of the Keys, just as Bahamian wreckers had been doing in earlier years.

Key West wreckers were kept reasonably honest by the federal court, but there was one glaring exception and he was young Jacob Housman. Bored with sailing his father's trading schooner from port to port on Long Island Sound, Housman, chilled by wintry winds, departed unannounced and aimed his father's craft for the Barbados. He ground onto a reef at Key West, had his ship repaired in the two-year-old city, turned to wrecking and soon was in trouble with others of his breed, with appraisers, and with the federal court.

After one of his more flagrant floutings of a judicial order, Housman sailed up to the uninhabited 11-acre Indian Key and there established himself as king of the island. He prospered enormously, attracted 20 other wreckers and their families, established a three street village, obtained a post office, married, built a mansion, opened the Tropical—the Keys' first resort hotel,

SOME 60 MILES west of Key West, the Florida Keys trail out into a cluster of islands—the Tortugas. Spanish discoverer Ponce de Leon called them "Las Tortugas"—the turtles—because of the large number of turtles there. During the early 1800s, the U.S. began a chain of seacoast defenses from Maine to Texas. On 16-acre Garden Key, construction began in 1846 on Fort Jefferson. Although construction continued for nearly thirty years, the fort was never finished. (L.C.)

DR. SAMUEL A. MUDD, one of the four "Lincoln conspirators" imprisoned at Fort Jefferson in 1865. Unaware that John Wilkes Booth had assassinated President Lincoln, he set Booth's leg which had been broken when he jumped from the Presidential Box at Ford's Theatre. The innocent physician was sentenced to life imprisonment, but after helping fight a yellow fever epidemic at the fort in 1867, and through petitions of his family, he was released in March 1869. (Mudd)

NED SPANGLER *(left)*, a stagehand at Ford's Theatre, was caught up in the conspiracy because he had stabled Booth's horses. Nearly one and a half years after his release he turned up at Dr. Mudd's home in Bryantown, Maryland where he lived until his death. SAMUEL ARNOLD *(center)*, worked as a store clerk outside Fort Monroe, Virginia, but Booth had involved him in an earlier plot to kidnap Lincoln. He was freed along with Spangler. MICHAEL O'LAUGHLIN, like Arnold, was drawn into the kidnap plot that fell through. He died of yellow fever in 1867 at Fort Jefferson. (LC)

and, in a masterful coup, gerrymandered creation of Dade County, carving from it enough of Monroe, (later restored) to remove him from jurisdiction of Key West courts and establish Indian Key as county seat.

When Seminole Indians began warring to the south and into the Everglades he even drew for his growing community the dubious protection of the Navy's Florida Squadron, a fleet of seven ships under command of Lt. Cmdr. John T. McLaughlin. The squadron distinguished itself by being missing the one time it was needed, and by spending more for "medicines" ($16,-000 a year) than all other units of the Navy combined. Congressional investigation revealed that "medicine" purchased by the squadron consisted solely of rum and fine wines.

Although both were New York-born, no island could be inhabited by two men less alike than Housman and Dr. Henry Perrine. A physician with a compulsive craving for knowledge, ill health forced Dr. Perrine from medicine and into a tropical climate. He became U.S. consul at the port of Campeche on Mexico's Yucatan peninsula. There he developed an interest in tropical plants and trees, and experimented with them for 13 years before seeking a place in south Florida where he could carry on his research. He chose Indian Key, arriving there with a wife and three children on Christmas Day of 1838.

He often left his plants and trees to treat the sick, including Seminoles who brought their ill and injured to the island. When word of Indian troubles reached Housman he, in contrast to Dr. Perrine's humanity, sought a government contract which would permit him to hunt and kill Seminoles at $200 a head. This was a mistake. Word of Housman's homicidal scheme reached Chief Chekika of the hostile Seminoles.

On August 7, 1840, the rum-loving Florida Squadron was on the Florida mainland investigating a false report of hostilities. At Tea Table Key, the squadron's base, only 15 sailors, 10 of them ailing, were left to tend the Navy depot. That night Chief Chekika and his warriors struck Indian Key to loot and burn every building except one—that of Postmaster Charles Howe. When razing of the island ended at dawn, 10 slaves and six of the 45 whites who had been on Indian Key were dead. One was Dr. Perrine. His wife and children escaped to the Tea Table Key where they were joined during the night and early morning by other survivors, including the Housmans.

Broke and defeated, Housman returned to Key West and penitently went to work as a mate on a former rival's salvage ship. Nine months after the Indian Key massacre he was killed while attempting to board a vessel aground in the Keys.

Since then Indian Key has been an occasional fishing camp, but today only readily visible evidence of the one-time community are the crumbling cisterns used to catch household water.

DUE WEST of Fort Jefferson is Loggerhead Key where the Dry Tortugas Lighthouse is located. . This 150-foot high conical tower was erected in 1858. The buildings nearby were used by the lighthouse keeper and his family. (MCPL)

JUDAH P. BENJAMIN, Secretary of State for the Confederate States of America, escaped federal pursuers in a boat from Knights Key near Marathon in June 1865. Pictured on this Confederate $2 bill, Benjamin hired a captain to take him from Knights Key up Hawk Channel to Indian Key and then to Bimini. He went on to England where he earned prominence for his "Treatise on the Law of Sales of Personal Property" in 1868.

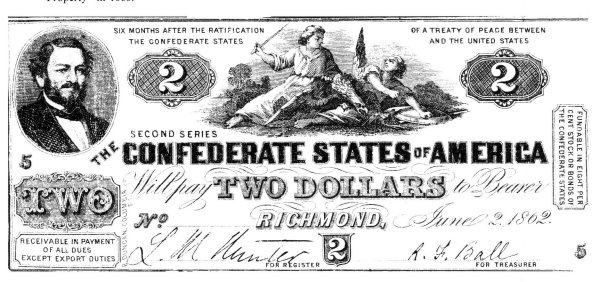

PIONEERS OF TAVERNIER—Amos and Ada Elizabeth (Eliza) Lowe. They were married August 27, 1859 and homesteaded after the 1882 land grant. They grew pineapples and limes. (Lowe)

In 1950 there were no more than a dozen homes, all rebuilt since the 1935 hurricane on Lower Matecumbe Key. Here, as on Upper Matecumbe and Windley Key were briefly those camps established for the "bonus army," World War I veterans who descended upon Washington in the waning years of Herbert Hoover's presidency. In camps in the Keys they were given room, good food, $30 to $45 a month, and put to work clearing land, building roads and in the first organized effort to control the mosquito population.

At least 200 of them lost their lives in the 1935 hurricane, and their camps were abandoned.

Damaged roads and bridges were rebuilt by a crew of 800 workmen in 1936 and, with a bond issue to be repaid through tolls, an entire road was finally bridged and opened to traffic in March 1938. The principal accomplishments in bridging open water were the construction of a bridge from Lower Matecumbe to Long Key, a two-sectioned span totaling 6,236 feet; the bridge 11,960 feet from Long Key to Conch Key; the spectacular 35,716 foot Seven-Mile Bridge from Knights Key to Little Duck Key; and the 5,356-foot Bahia Honda Bridge linking the Key of that name with West Summerland.

Crossing in 1950 from Lower Matecumbe, the visitor found the bridge to what was called Greyhound Key interrupted by a tiny parcel of island known as Poor Old Craig's Key. Poor Old Craig was R. W. Craig, and regardless of the appearance the unpredictable Keys character presented, he was definitely not poor. Craig grew wealthy in land speculation and other investments.

Craig Key was once occupied by fishermen whose homes projected over the water.which were destroyed however, in the 1935 hurricane. Older residents recalled that late in the 1920s President Hoover anchored his yacht off Craig during a Keys visit, but no one was unduly impressed, for the islands have

26

long been a haven and temporary escape for the great and near great. In 1950, as he had done at various times, Poor Old Craig operated a grocery, restaurant, and bar on the picturesque Key.

The tip of Long Key had in mid-century become Greyhound Key. Bought by the Greyhound Corporation in 1936, it had a post house for refreshment of bus passengers and other travelers, some tourist accommodations and an imposing stone residence that provided a home for the facility's manager. Southwest, at the opposite end of Long Key, the traveler passed an area once operated as the Long Key Fishing Camp, a resort facility built by Flagler when his railraod arrived here. Zane Grey was one of its more renowned and frequent visitors. It, too, was destroyed in the 1935 hurricane, along with most of the coconut palms which, until then, gave Long Key the densest growth of these graceful, tropical trees except, perhaps, in undeveloped areas of Upper Matecumbe.

Early in 1906 a major fish kill occurred on Long Key, the cause being a phenomenom rare, but not unrecorded, in the Middle and Upper Keys. Fish were killed by freezing or near freezing temperatures. Readings were not recorded on Long Key, but in Tavernier the mercury reportedly dropped to 31 in this otherwise frost-free section of the nation. That was a year of disaster, for nine months later, on October 17 and 18, a hurricane ripped Long Key where railroad laborers were concentrated while building the bridge to Conch Key. Most men were housed in floating barges carrying two-story living quarters. These were known as quarterboats. Men ashore, and those on all barges except one, survived the storm. Quarterboat No. 4 broke loose from its moorings and was carried into the Atlantic with 175 workers, including 50 new laborers who arrived the day the hurricane began. The boat broke up in heavy seas and only 72 of the men aboard were rescued.

First land reached after crossing the 11,960-foot Long Key Bridge is Conch Key, a tiny island newcomers persist in referring to as quaint. Uninhabited until 1925, frame homes built then on lots only 25 to 40 feet wide are stilted over water with boat docks extending still farther into salt water. After 1925 it was home to many commercial fishermen, but in mid-century its population of 50 was divided between the professionals and those more recently arrived retirees intent on spending their remaining days with a rod and reel in hand and a boat rocking beneath them.

Following Conch Key, just offshore, is Duck Key, inhabited for a few years in the late 1820s and early 1830s when Charleston, S. C., investors financed development of ponds for drying of salt. The venture failed when owners found it netting only modest profits, but in 1950 plans were in the making to build a causeway to connect Duck Key to U.S. 1, and to construct a resort there.

Across another bridge lies Grassy Key, dotted on its northern end with proliferating fishing camps. Once a part of the Vaca Keys, the island received an identity of its own from railroad engineers who crossed this way in 1908. Grassy drew occasional farming families in the early 1800s, but when a census was taken in 1870, only Samuel and Sirena Jenkins, a young South Carolina couple with a son, James, were living there. Coming of the railroad brought construction of a hotel and several homes for workers. A few remained behind to plant key lime groves when the railroad moved on to what is now Marathon. Population did not exceed 50 until post-war years when new arrivals came slowly and in small numbers to retire, operate fishing camps and other tourist accommodations.

Crawl Key is indistinguishable from Grassy, however, upon reaching Marathon a traveler passes the busiest home construction activity thus far in the Keys.

Here in Marathon, still commonly called Key Vaca, nearly 1,000 residents were settled in 1950 with more arriving, some drawn by Keys climate, others by the bonefishing which centers here, still others by business and employment opportunities.

Capt. Anthony Pent and his father, William, both born on Key Vaca, report that their ancestors arrived about 1800. Members of the family later farmed and fished on Bamboo, an isolated Key in Florida Bay, and 16 Pents were there in 1870. Members of the Russell family are recorded in the late 1820s, and indications that a settlement existed is found in a letter written by Dr. Perrine, victim of the Indian Key massacre, a few months before his death in 1840. The letter asks a New York friend to subscribe to a farming publication for benefit of the children "of the Bahamian school in Key Vaca." It is probable that Marathon's growing black community began with a Bahamian Negro couple name Rigby who came in the 1890s. They ultimately populated the island with 20 children.

The railroad began regular service to Marathon and deep water docks at Knights Key in 1908, and for six years it was a center for construction workers and engineers. An estimated 50,000 men worked on building the railroad, seldom more than 5,000 at one time. When Marathon became the hub of activity, many were quartered there as crews worked north from Key West and south from Knights Key. Shops were on Boot Key, bridged from Marathon.

It is claimed the railroad brought Marathon its name, when, after the 1906 hurricane damaged rails and bridges already constructed, Flagler considered abandonment of the project but finally sent engineers instructions to keep building. An unknown workman is reputed to have commented, "This is getting to be a real marathon." and the name stuck.

This reported christening tests one's reason yet it still persists. A similar problem exists with Cudjoe Key, lying farther to the south. Since no one has come up with a more plausible story, it is reluctantly accepted that an early farmer there was named Joe and he had a cousin in Key West with a speech impediment. The Key West cousin was prone to visit Joe and he announced his departures with tangled diction in which he said he was going to visit "Cud Joe." There is still debate whether emphasis is given the first or second syllable.

Aside from offering rows of bunkhouses where laborers received "three squares" and a bed along with their $1.25 a day, Marathon's chief railroad attraction was the paymaster who was headquartered there. Although the abstemious Flagler decreed there be no strong drink in his worker's camps, the order was as effective as one banning hurricanes would have been.

When the mass of workers reached Marathon they were wont, on paydays, to crowd aboard any sea-going craft and descend upon Key West, a city advertised far and wide as having more saloons than churches, and where practitioners of the oldest profession outnumbered clergy 10 to 1. Although the fortunate Key Westers hadn't known a tropical storm of consequence in 60 years, these railroad workers are reputed to have provided them with a reasonable facsimile.

In the cause of municipal salvation, county seat merchants felt it prudent to take essential pleasures to the workers rather than put them to the trouble of a 47-mile trip. So each payday an interesting flotilla sailed from Key West to Marathon. In the lead were those merchants bearing products rated 80 proof or better, next came the patent medicine men who carried nostrums high in alcoholic content. Since the professional ladies were more alluring when seen through boozy eyes than through those stone sober, they followed three hours behind the first contingent. And behind them came itinerant evangelists with a boatload of whatever choir singers, tract peddlers, cornet players, and drum beaters they could enlist.

Once the railroad moved on, the population of Marathon dwindled to its former state, this being approximately nothing. If a 1950 visitor inquired, "Who's in charge here?" the obvious answer would have been realtor, developer, and commercial fish buyer, W.A. Parrish Sr., who did not arrive until 1927. His daughter, Mrs. Harry Snow, Sr., recalls that when she arrived with her parents and five brothers and sisters, the family more than doubled the community's population. She naturally recalls the presence there of Harry Snow, keeper of the railroad's water tower. She married him. Then there was a section foreman and his one employee, and the station agent. The Kyle family was encamped on Pigeon Key which was no more than a speck of land supporting the Seven-Mile Bridge.

Leaving Marathon, a traveler would cross the Seven-Mile Bridge and then a five-mile chain of mostly uninhabited small Keys ending on Big Pine Key. Relief from the bustle of Marathon would be found in a slow drive skirting the Atlantic on Bahia Honda Key. It is here that the smooth, sunlit water of the ocean spectrum from mauve pink and lavender through creamy grey, milk green, and every shade of blue imaginable. Even the clouds have reflected un-

BUILT ON Plantation Key in 1885, the *Island Home* was a main link between the Upper Keys and the outside World. A two-masted, 44-ton schooner, the vessel carried produce to Key West and Miami where it picked up food, mail and supplies. John (Johnny Brush) Pinder had the *Island Home* built primarily to carry pineapples and limes. (Fontis)

dersides of blue-green. This array of color is created by the soil composition, vegetation, and depth of the sea bottom, and the spectrum constantly changes with the shifting sun.

Although the highway crosses it in less than three miles, Big Pine is one of the larger Florida Keys in total acreage. It is unusual in that, as its name implies, it is forested with a southern pine.

First settled by fisherman, long-time residents of the sparsely settled Key had seen varied attempts at exploitation over the years. Spongers had been active along its shores, and in 1950 William (Sonny) Larson was still a familiar figure poling his skiff and wielding his three-pronged fork. A plant to extract shark liver oil came and went as did other enterprises related to the surrounding sea. Cattle breeding and dairying failed when mosquitoes and horseflies weakened the animals. So the land was turned into developements, and by 1950 one-acre lots were bringing as much as $200.

Across from Big Pine on the Torch Keys, a bar catered to fishermen living in the few homes lining the channel in 1950. On to the south was solid mangrove covering land once cleared for unsuccessful farming ventures. There was, in fact, little to distract the motorist until arrival on Sugarloaf Key.

Sugarloaf drew attention of Dr. H. F. Moore, head of the U.S. Bureau of Fisheries, who established a small station here in 1901 to experiment in controlled raising of sponges. He was aided by Ralph M. Munroe, know as the the commodore, who conducted similar experiments on Elliott Key, and by Jeremy Fogarty, a Key West sponge buyer. The cultivation process was simple, consisting of cutting a small section from a live adult sponge, attaching it to stone or cement and then placing the cutting into a controlled bed of water. Experimenters, who included Key West physician, Dr. J. V. Harris, found

30

that approximately 75 percent of the "planted" cuttings matured. Fogarty, however, complained that spongers soon learned of the controlled areas and pirated mature sponges unless constant supervision could be given.

Five years after Moore began his experiments, Charles W. Chase, a British theatrical producer, was left stranded in Key West with his troupe. Notwithstanding the unlikely merger of the theatre with sponging, Chase heard of Moore's research, became interested and enlisted support of his brother, George, and another Londoner, Henry Bate, in buying property from Dr. Harris and then erecting the Florida Sponge and Fruit Company in Sugarloaf. By 1912, a small town surrounded the plant in which sponges were planted and harvested on an assembly line basis. It was, of course, named Chase. Chase's son, Pete, was made a deputy sheriff and charged with driving off the poachers. He would later join Carl Fisher in promotion and development of Miami Beach. Meanwhile more than 100 workers manned the sponge plant and lived in homes built for them. There was also an ice plant producing 300 blocks of that rare and precious commodity. In 1913, the company, with its sponges in high demand, decided to hold off the harvest for one year to allow greater growth and even greater profit. Chase and his associates failed to anticipate the outbreak of World War I a few months later. Company funds were in a London bank and, with start of the war, England froze all foreign assets.

Suddenly without capital, Florida Sponge and Fruit was bankrupt. In an attempt to stave off disaster, Chase enlisted the Tatum Brothers, a Miami Beach realty firm, to sell shares in Florida Sponge and Fruit to northern investors wintering in Florida. The brothers assigned the task to their top real estate salesman, R. C. Perky, who found financiers disinterested in sponge culture, but extremely interested in Florida land. So when Chase's firm went into bankruptcy in 1919, Perky bought almost all of Sugarloaf for a mere $10,000, turned it into a real estate development, and changed the name to Perky. He should have stuck to sponges, for the subdivisions drew no buyers, chiefly because, at the time, Sugarloaf was cursed with the peskiest mosquito population in the Keys.

Perky's unusual, and final, attempt to evict the bloodthirsty insects resulted in construction of his only memorial. It had its origins in his recollection that where there are flying bats there are no mosquitoes. The would-be developer investigated to determine the type of a home that would be most pleasing to bats and decided on a louvered wooden tower, reminiscent of those supporting Holland's windmills. So Perky built his dark and shingled tower to a height of 35 feet and then sought a supplier who could furnish unlimited numbers of bats.

It would brighten history to report, as legend does, that Perky located his bats and, amid celebration and fanfare, released them only to have the winged rodents fly north and disappear forever. Although some old-timers will insist that this is indeed what happened, there is no evidence beyond legend to indicate any bat saw the inside of the bat tower.

As Perky's fortunes dwindled, he tried operating a fishing camp and failed, his home burned, and other buildings were ravaged by time, neglect, and termites.

Perky died, and during World War II one of the buildings he had owned operated as a bar and dancehall of dubious repute. When the war ended, the property was purchased for future development by Radford Crane.

At the north end of the island there opened in 1930 Pirates Cove, built by C. Irving Wright, a Massachusetts manufacturer. It was a resort complex with lodge, private cottages, swimming pool, a fishing camp, and a restaurant judged to be dispenser of the finest food in the Keys. In 1948 most of the buildings were destroyed by a small but vicious hurricane. The resort was not rebuilt.

Leaving Sugarloaf, a motorist crosses Keys mostly known as the Saddlebunches, a cluster of more than 100 small mangrove islands, uninhabited in mid-century, the loftiest rising no more than three feet above high tide. Only 10 are linked by the highway's bridges.

Boca Chica Key, just nine miles from downtown Key West, gives indication of its use in sight and sound long before the motorist reaches it. Once offering a beach that was the mecca for holidaying Key Westers, the Navy in World War II installed a busy naval air station there, adding military strength to that which had existed since 1823 at the Key West Naval Station.

Before entering Key West, the motorist visits Stock Island, named for livestock once kept there awaiting slaughter for the Key West market. The island structures have been in highly diverse use. Identified with Stock Island far and wide was Mom's Tea Room, an establishment that definitely sold no tea. Mom, whose name was Rose Rabin, ran, under the approving noses of the Navy and Monroe County authorities, one of the most successful fancy houses in the history of prostitution. During World War II it was proclaimed as the principal attraction in Key West, then known as the Singapore of the West.

In late war years, Navy officers, in the cause of Navy Relief, borrowed Mom's girls for a fund-raising soiree, and word of the affair, reported to have gotten somewhat out of hand, reached Drew Pearson who offered an account of the bawdy event in his nationally syndicated column. End of Mom's.

Nearby, however, the 1950 motorist could find a bar where a few of Mom's former hirelings were known to linger. Also on Stock Island were fishing facilities and Monroe County General Hospital.

Still farming in 1950 was H. Dexter Hubel, who planted his first crop on Key Biscayne in 1880, then tried farming the Torch Keys before moving to No Name and finally, in 1925, to Stock Island.

A 1950 visitor entered Key West on North Roosevelt Boulevard, one of its

KEY WEST was a bustling seaport in the 1880s, and some families moved up the Keys seeking more breathing space and opportunities for fishing, sponging, and farming.

few wide thoroughfares, and immediately he was in a city that is of the Keys, but not like the Keys. Except for fishing, nothing previously learned along all of the Keys would have validity here. In all of the "outside" Keys the people were Anglo-Saxon in speech, appearance and character and most of the homes they built were midwestern. Life for pioneers was rigid and distinctly puritan. In Key West the rules no longer applied.

Its character was Latin, its appearance, New England. The food was Conch-cum-Spanish, attitudes tolerant. Sin in the Upper Keys became a minor vice in Key West. It had another, and very different, story to tell.

If a traveler feels impelled to follow the Keys to their final outpost it is in Key West where he parks his car and takes to the air or water. Westward lie the islands of Boca Grande and the Marquesas, the former showing stilt fishermen's homes built in shallow water, the latter boasting a single quarter-moon shaped island with one of the finest Keys beaches. The remaining islands of the Marquesas are scarcely above high tide, and are chiefly sanctuaries.

Beyond, and 60 miles from Key West, are the Dry Tortugas, a cluster of tiny outpost islands offering just one of special interest. This is Garden Key, site of historic Fort Jefferson. In 1846 work was begun there on the hexagonal fortress, built of brick enclosing 16 acres, and with parapets planned for 450 cannon rising 50 feet above the moat. The fort, never completed, heard no shot fired in anger, but rather received it principal attention when those convicted of conspiracy in the assassination of Abraham Lincoln were imprisoned there after the Civil War, a war that had little effect on the Keys.

Those outside Key West were too few, too busy, and too far from communication to give the war more than passing attention. Key West remained in Union control, a condition that aroused little temper. Best known Tortugas prisoner was Dr. Samuel A. Mudd, imprisoned for setting John Wilkes Booth's broken leg. The fort was abandoned in 1874, revived as an auxiliary to the Key West seaplane base in World War I, and as an observation post in World War II. In 1935 it was declared a National Monument and continues as an attraction to visitors, guided and watched over by rangers of the National Park Service.

In 1950 a visitor would have noted in daytime an ever increasing number of anchored shrimp boats. At dark these moved to nearby beds of the newly located night-feeding large pink shrimp. The new find was destined to make shrimping immensely profitable and give new vigor to the economy of Key West and Marathon, home ports for many boats.

This was the first of many changes the sage of 1950 would foresee for the Florida Keys—especially those outside Key West—in coming decades. In actual growth, the figure reached would be well above that predicted in 1950, and with this would come problems unimagined by the wisest 1950 resident. And even the clairvoyant would not envision the pendulum, which in still the next decade would swing in an opposite direction—one aimed at holding fast to what is here while catching up to what has happened.

USING a glassbottom bucket, a Keys sponger spots the valuable marine animal on the bottom and pulls the sponge up with a long-handled, three-pronged hook. Sponge were sold in Key West. (MCPL)

The Florida Keys from 1900 to 1930

TRAVELING by sailboat, Milton Knowles of Key West tended the kerosene-fueled beacons along Hawk Channel in the Lower Keys in the early 1900s. Hawk Channel lies inside the reef and was the protected route used by Keys residents. (Knowles)

PLANTER, just above Tavernier, was close to deep water for shipping and became a major pineapple producing community. A post office was established here in December, 1891. The 1909 hurricane damaged many homes, and with the coming of the railroad, the population shifted toward Tavernier. The large two-story home in the center is where Sam and Caroline Johnson, two of the earliest settlers, lived. (MCPL)

ANOTHER HOME in the Planter community. Planter once occupied land used today as Harry Harris County Park. (MCPL)

THE *Island Home* tied up in the Miami River. Men in the photograph from left are Dolphus Sawyer, _____ Pinder, the owner John (Johnny Brush) Pinder, George Albury, and Jimmy Pinder. Brush Pinder sold the *Island Home* in the early 1920s to a Miami businessman. Renamed the *Madan*, the ship was captured in March, 1926, and her illegal cargo of 1,800 cases of liquor and 600 cases of alcohol seized by the U.S. Coast Guard. (MCPL)

REALIZING the geographical and financial advantage of having the closest railroad to the Panama Canal, Henry M. Flagler, president of the Florida East Coast Railway, gave the "go ahead" sign to extend his railroad from Homestead to Key West in 1904. At Jewfish Creek in the Upper Keys, the railroad set up one of its material yards in 1906 to supply the crews working "on the grade" down the Keys.

OLD ENGINE No. 30 with its wooden-slatted cowcatcher pauses in Tavernier. Engineer Rube Goethe, left, later became the man behind the throttle of the *Havana Special* on the Key West to Miami run. No. 30 was used to haul supplies when this photograph was taken around 1906. The 1897-vintage engine was built by the Schenectady (N'Y') Locomotive Works. (Lowe)

LOOKING NORTHWARD from the recently completed Tavernier Creek trestle around 1906.

LABORERS of many nationalities worked on making Flagler's dream become a reality. Some were hired in New York City, and the railroad paid their fare down, but it had to be reimbursed. Many Key Westers also joined the crew. Here a track gang pauses at the Islamorada siding.

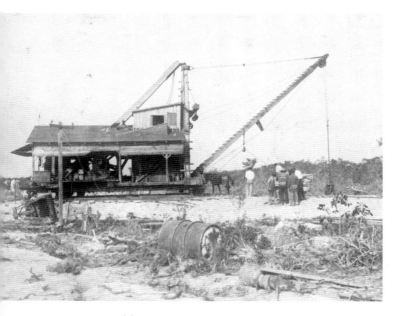

EXCAVATOR No. 1 bites up buckets of marl to build the grade on Lower Matecumbe. This excavator later blew up and burned.

SMOKE rises from a dredge working to fill the gap between Upper and Lower Matecumbe. This fill is located beside Indian Key Channel.

RAILROAD right-of-way cuts through the heart of Long Key. The coconut trees had been planted over the years as a business venture by various owners. The marker at right was used by railroad surveyor in 1905.

RARE PHOTOGRAPH of an early train wreck on Lower Matecumbe Key August 12, 1907. Engine No. 20 and tender are shown turned on their side as the crew prepares to right the train. The train was used by the work crew and no one is known to have been killed in the accident. (Ley)

MERLIN ALBURY, who became postmaster of Tavernier in 1916, was photographed on Long Key about the time construction began in 1905. (Ley)

THE ALBURY CLAN, 17 of them, after church in 1907 at the home pf William and Ada Albury. They had attended the nearby Tavernier Methodist Church. Prior to the railroad, families from Planter sailed down to Tavernier for church. (Ley)

FAMILIES in the Upper Keys used to hitch rides on the supply train to attend church in Tavernier. Mostly Alburys, they pose beside Engine No. 201 on a siding. Small boy (second from right) is Capt. Eugene Lowe. The wooden tanks were used to haul fresh water to work crews. (Lowe)

DRESSED in Sunday finery, Upper Keys residents prepare to go to church in 1910. (Ley)

FARMER AND FISHERMAN, Beauregard Albury was one of the most colorful men of the Upper Keys. With a red rose in his lapel, he poses with his wife, Mamie Pinder Albury, in the Key West studio of photographer A. J. Estevez. His parents were from the Bahamas originally, and they settled on Key Largo in 1886 to raise fruit and vegetables. (Lowe)

THE RAILROAD had pushed its way through Long Key in 1906. Mule-drawn carts carried fill dug from the shore of Long Key to build up the nearby railroad grade. (Key)

LABORERS WORKING on the Long Key Viaduct enjoyed the luxury of living ashore in screened barracks. After the railroad was completed, some buildings were kept as cabins for the Long Key Fishing Camp. (Key)

AN OVERLOADED LAUNCH ferries men from Long Key to work on the viaduct. (Key)

ENGINE No. 10 was one of the Florida East Coast Railway's ancient locomotives that had run on the Jacksonville, St. Augustine, and Halifax line. It was used as a work engine on the construction to Long Key and barged to Marathon in November, 1907. (Key)

TAKEN from atop a pile driver, this view shows an early phase of construction on the Long Key Viaduct. The pilings were used to secure cofferdams.

FORMS for the arches span the completed piers. Arch forms rested on pilings, and the piers had been built in individual cofferdams in which the steel-enforced concrete was poured. The Long Key Viaduct required 286,000 barrels of cement, 177,000 cubic yards of crushed rock, 106,000 cubic yards of sand, 612,000 feet of piling, 5,700 tons of reinforcing rods, and 26 million feet of dressed lumber.

SIDE BY SIDE, the arches formed the Long Key Viaduct *(above)*. The engineering marvel with 186 arches spans nearly two and a quarter miles of water. After a hard day's work, laborers gather outside a mess hall for the dinner gong to sound *(below)*.

THE STERNWHEELER *Virginia* unloads a cargo of dynamite at one of the work camps. Eight Mississippi River steamers were imported for work in the shallow waters of the Keys.

WHEN THE RAILWAY construction forces arrived on Key Vaca in early 1906, they found several families on the bayside opposite Rachel Key. Carlton J. Corliss, who worked in the railroad's Marathon accounting office, later wrote about the history of the area and told how one of the families "by the name of Rigby consisted of a man, his wife and 20 children." (Corliss)

A DEVASTATING HURRICANE in September, 1909 washed out more than 40 miles of embankment and track in the Upper Keys, and flipped this Marathon home over on its side. Belatedly heeding the warning of Conchs about plugging up natural water gaps between the islands, engineers revised plans, and added 18 miles of bridges. (Corliss)

A PIONEER FAMILY of Key Vaca about 1910. (HASF)

FIRST PHYSICIAN and surgeon on Key Vaca, Dr. Edward R. (Doc) Lowe was in charge of the railroad's emergency hospital. Doc Lowe is on the left holding a stem of bananas. The man on the right is identified as Frank, an island native. The doctor was also called Judge Lowe after his appointment about 1909 as the first justice of the peace for the third district of Monroe County. The district included all of the Florida Keys except the city of Key West. (Corliss)

HORSE-POWERED CARTS hauled large rocks to the "Hell Hole Fill" across "Pull-and-Be-Damned Creek." The fill linked Crawl Key and the eastern end of Key Vaca.

THIS DOCK in Marathon was the main transfer point in 1910 supplying construction camps to the south and west of Marathon. It was located to the rear of where the greater Marathon Chamber of Commerce building is today. The long building at left is a mess hall. (Corliss)

THE RAILWAY DOCK connected to the mainline in the distance. The large building at right is Marathon's first hotel. Built by the railway company, the Marathon Hotel opened in the winter of 1908-09 under the management of Mrs. E. J. DeVore. The waterfront area is where the Marathon Yacht Club is today. (Corliss)

MARATHON'S first athletic club was organized in February, 1913 with Carlton J. Corliss as president. This is the club's bathhouse and dock which were located just a short distance from the mess hall. (Corliss)

RAILROAD office workers at Knights Key dock rest on kegs of Budweiser beer. (Corliss)

KEY WEST, CUBA AND THE WEST INDIES

Knights Key---Key West---Havana Line

(Touching at Key West)

Effective from Knights Key, Florida, Sunday, April 2nd, 1911

Lv. Knights Key,	Sundays,	Tuesdays,	Thursdays,	12 00 Noon
Ar. Key West,	Sundays,	Tuesdays,	Thursdays,	4 00 P. M.
Lv. Key West,	Sundays,	Tuesdays,	Thursdays,	6 00 P. M.
Ar. Havana,	Mondays,	Wednesdays,	Fridays,	7 30 A. M.
Lv. Havana,	Mondays,	Wednesdays,	Fridays,	4 00 P. M.
Ar. Key West,	Tuesdays,	Thursdays,	Saturdays,	5 30 A. M.
Lv. Key West,	Tuesdays,	Thursdays,	Saturdays,	7 30 A. M.
Ar. Knights Key,	Tuesdays,	Thursdays,	Saturdays,	11 30 A. M

Additional Sailings Between Key West and Havana

Lv. Key West,	Mondays,	Fridays,	8 00 P. M.
Ar. Havana,	Tuesdays,	Saturdays,	6 30 A. M.
Lv. Havana,	Tuesdays,	Saturdays,	12 00 Noon
Ar. Key West,	Tuesdays,	Saturdays,	8 00 P. M.

FLAGLER traveled in the first train to go over the Long Key Viaduct and down to Knights Key dock when the rails were connected January 22, 1908. This was four years to the day before he rode his private car "Rambler" over the completed extension to Key West. Passenger service officially began February 5, 1908 as shown in this photograph of the train crossing Long Key Viaduct. (Fontis)

A TIMETABLE of 1910. Knights Key dock was the southern terminus of the extension until the line was completed to Key West. Train passengers could catch a steamship to Key West and even go on to Havana, Cuba. (Fontis)

THE *Miami* of the Peninsular and Occidental Steamship Company (P. & O.) at Knights Key dock. (Corliss)

PACE JOHNSON and his family along with Newton Pinder prepare to set out in a small sailboat. The family lived on Key Largo. (Albury)

THE HOME of John (Johnny Brush) Pinder on Plantation Key. Just beside this house, Pinder built his famous schooner, the *Island Home.* (Albury)

WATER to quench the thirst of railroad workmen and to supply the locomotives was hauled down on flat-cars. The cypress tanks each held about 7,000 gallons—a month's supply was about 4.5 million gallons. The water train shown here is crossing the Long Key Viaduct.

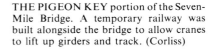

LOOKING toward Pigeon Key, a portion of the Seven-Mile Bridge takes shape. The bridge was built in four sections—Knights Key Bridge, Pigeon Key Bridge, Moser Channel Bridge, and Pacet Channel Viaduct. Bridges were built on piers; viaducts used arches. (Corliss)

THE PIGEON KEY portion of the Seven-Mile Bridge. A temporary railway was built alongside the bridge to allow cranes to lift up girders and track. (Corliss)

IMPRESSED with government experiments in sponge cultivation at Sugarloaf Key, Englishman Charles W. Chase purchased the property from Dr. J. V. Harris in 1909. Renamed Chase, it had grown into a small community by 1911. The tower on the right was used to guard the sponge crop from possible poachers. (Stricker)

PERHAPS IT WAS Chase's theatrical background that prompted him to build this wishing well at the sponge farming center. (Stricker)

DR. HARRIS had built a three bedroom home six feet above the ground on Sugarloaf Key before he sold it to Chase. (Stricker)

TENNIS, ANYONE? Carlton J. Corliss (far left) met the young lady in the photograph, Miss Loretta Billings, when she came to Marathon in the spring of 1913 to visit relatives. They were married a few months later and honeymooned in Cuba. On the night they returned, friends built a large bonfire on the shore near the tennis court and workmen serenaded them with mandolins and guitars. (Corliss)

NICHOLAS MATCOVICH, a recluse on No Name Key, peers from the door of his driftwood house. W. J. Krome (dark suit), chief engineer on the railroad, and Mrs. Krome *(left)* visited Matcovich to buy sapodillas around 1912. He homesteaded 320 acres on No Name Key and died August 14, 1919 at 92 years of age. (Matcovich)

ALFRED (Bubba Smart) Atchison of Key West was one of the last of the master wreckers. When wrecking dwindled, Bubba Smart went into pineapple growing on Elliott Key. This photograph of his first shipment of pineapples was taken around 1910 on Key Largo. (Galey)

THE RAILROAD OFFICE at Bahia Honda Key. In the photograph are Charles Leach, Ada Munson, unknown, Ted Bayly, and Mr. and Mrs. Light. (Bayly)

MANY A WHEELBARROW of marl went into the making of this grade on Big Pine Key. Judging by the curve, it was probably just south of Spanish Harbor.

ON A DAY OFF from railroad construction, Mr. and Mrs. Light enjoyed exploring the Lower Florida Keys. He was an employee of the railroad. (Bayly)

MAP SHOWS Key West extension of the Florida East Coast Railway.

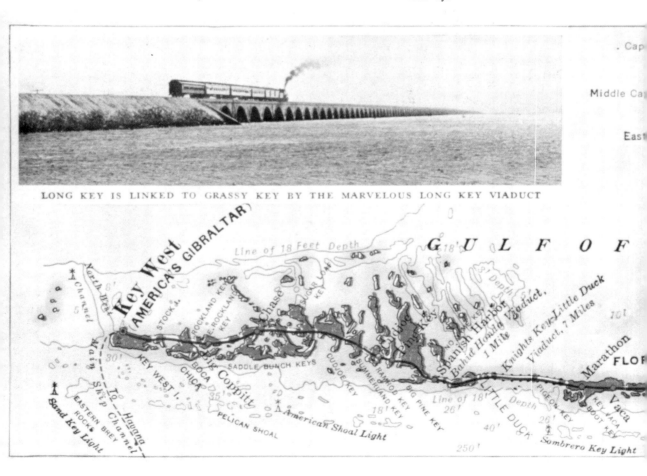

LONG KEY IS LINKED TO GRASSY KEY BY THE MARVELOUS LONG KEY VIADUCT

USED AS A MESS HALL during railroad construction on Big Pine Key, this building was bought by Copeland Johnson of Key West who used it for family outings. He is shown in the white shirt on the porch about 1920. Before World War II, the then-Senator Harry S. Truman spent a week here fishing and playing poker. (MCPL)

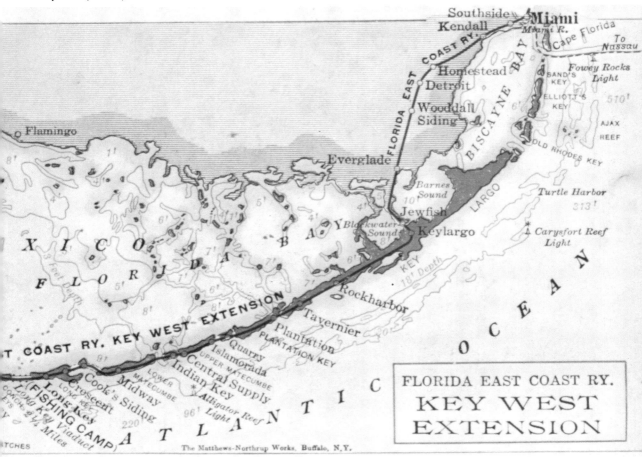

SAND KEY LIGHT and Weather Station about seven miles from Key West. A hurricane destroyed the weather station, but the light still guides ships along the reef. (Stricker)

FIRST PUBLIC SCHOOL at Tavernier around 1914. Eugene Lowe, top left, recalls that the one room school house provided classes for grades 1 through 8. The teacher in the center is Elise Warren from Key West. (Ley)

ZANE GREY, famous author of western novels and an avid sportsman, wears his sun helmet as he stands beside a catch of three amberjack and a barracuda at the Long Key Fishing Camp about 1916. His brother and frequent fishing companion, R. C. Grey, is on the right. One of the writer's hobbies was photography, and he took this picture by tripping a timing device on the shutter and slipping back to pose with his brother. This photograph is from a glass negative discovered in the attic of Zane Grey's home in Lackawaxen, Pennsylvania. (Courtesy George Reiger and the Zane Grey Inn)

FAMILY CEMETERY plot on Islamorada located near present day Cheeca Lodge. The angel marks the grave of Etta Delores Pinder—born July 19, 1899, died February 21, 1914—the only child of Ella and Bramin Pinder. (Albury)

COVER of a brochure which explains the various fishing contests held yearly by members of the Long Key Fishing Club. The club was organized in March 1917, and noted western author Zane Grey served as its first president. (Anderson)

1917 - 1918

LONG KEY
FISHING CLUB
LONG KEY, FLORIDA

TO DEVELOP THE BEST AND FINEST TRAITS OF SPORT, TO RESTRICT THE KILLING OF FISH, TO EDUCATE THE INEXPERIENCED ANGLER BY HELPING HIM, AND TO PROMOTE GOOD FELLOWSHIP

FISHING CLUB members and guests stayed in bungalows nestled among the coconut palms on Long Key. The camp itself was operated by the Flagler East Coast Hotel System. (Anderson)

THE LODGE at Long Key Fishing Camp was located on the ocean surrounded by a sandy beach. A tunnel beneath the railroad tracks made it more convenient for guests arriving by yachts on the bayside to travel to the lodge and bungalows. (Anderson)

WELL-DRESSED GUESTS *(above)* line the porch of the lodge at Long Key Fishing Camp. The lobby of the lodge was decorated with mounted fish, stuffed animals, and birds. (Anderson)

BOY SCOUTS of Key West Troop 5 on their Big Pine Key encampment in December 1921. A donkey peers out from the formation of Scouts on the left. The donkey was probably used as a "beast of burden" by some farmer on the Key. (Knowles)

A SUITCASE rests beside the railroad track as photographs are taken of a couple and their son before leaving Marathon. The station was located directly across from what is today the office of the Greater Marathon Chamber of Commerce. (Anderson)

OVERALL VIEW of Marathon around 1924 showing the station in the center. U. S. 1 today follows the path of the railroad tracks and this would be looking east. (Anderson)

LIKE MANY of the early settlers on the Keys, Edney Parker raised a large family. His father, William H., settled on Plantation Key in 1898 and reared eight children. Edney farmed, worked for the railroad, served as first mate on a freight packetship, served on a U. S. Customs Launch, and in later years was a bridge tender. Shown in this family photograph around 1925 are Etta (Sweeting), his wife Edna holding Franklin, Yvonne (Broomfield), Edney holding Sam, and Lois (Gaskin). Standing in the rear is Janice (Gentry). Later, five more children were born—Earl, Norman, Nolan, Faye, and Barbara. (Sweeting)

POSING OUTSIDE the Tavernier Post Office is postmaster Merlin Albury, his wife Jeanette and Lillian R. Sexton, postmistress at Key Largo. Older couple on right is not identified. Daniel W. Riley was the first postmaster when the Tavernier Post Office was established March 9, 1911. With his resignation that same month, however, the post office was closed and not reopened until January 21, 1916 when Albury took over. (Albury)

A MIAMI COUPLE who edited *Tropic Magazine* visited No Name Key in 1925 after purchasing land sight unseen. Mr. and Mrs. LeBaron Perrine found this aged caretaker, Uncle Tim, living on the desolate Key. He tied paper sacks around the grapes to protect them from birds. (Perrine)

BEFORE RETURNING to Miami, the Perrines visited the shark factory on Big Pine Key. Located on the Spanish Harbor side of the island, the factory turned out shark hides which were sold to a New Jersey firm, Ocean Leather Co. (Perrine)

A SHARK FISHERMAN repairs nets ripped by a sawfish. Possibly the first industry on Big Pine Key, the factory closed in the late 1930s. (Perrine)

64

AFTER THE HURRICANE of 1919, Dexter Hubel was one of the few who remained on No Name Key. He sold his property in 1925 to the Perrines and settled on Stock Island. This photograph was taken shortly after the 70-year old Hubel began clearing land for a new home on Stock Island. (Perrine)

MIAMI PHOTOGRAPHER Claude Matlack traveled to Key West on this motorized handcar in December, 1926. Matlack stopped frequently on his photographic journey to record life along the railroad. Utility wires were strung on both sides of the Long Key Viaduct. (HASF—Matlack)

146-40

The Over-Sea Highway, Once Termed A "F
To An Earl

The sharp urging of the muleteer as he clatters along in the interminable pr
bearing, the coming and going of the labor shifts—in short, all of the noises of Indus
the progress already made encourages one to believe that the time is not far distant wh

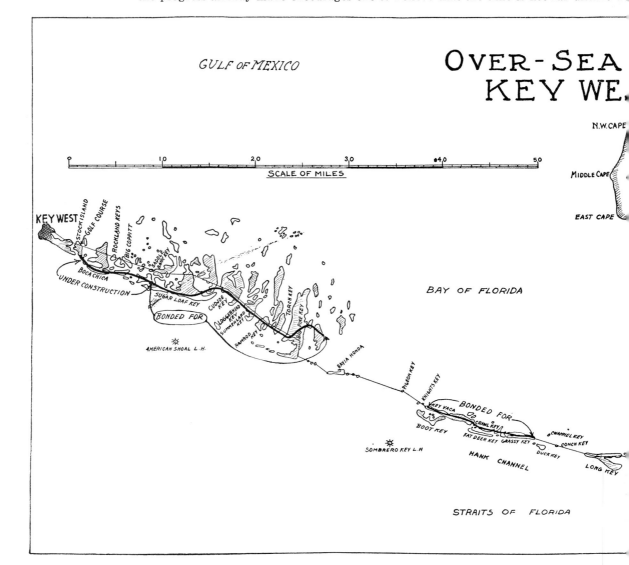

FACTS AND FIGURES

Contracts for thirteen miles of the highway have been let and work on this
of two sections of the highway simultaneously from each terminal so that as funds bec
comes an unbroken stretch of asphalt from the mainland to Key West. $2,600,000 w
the wherewithal to complete the remainder of the Over-Sea Highway, except for two
bridged and will very likely be financed through franchises granted to private capital
running at a schedule that will not impede travel, so that the motorist who breakfasts

A PROMOTIONAL BROCHURE on the "Over-Sea Highway." Anxious for a share in the land boom,
Monroe County citizens approved—with only two dissenting votes—a $2.5 million bond issue on March
12, 1926 to launch construction of the highway. Key West Police Chief Joseph W. Albury sent out a

)ream" Now An Actuality, Fast Progressing
npletion.

ourden-carriers, the monotonous song of the dredge shovels in their endless cycle of dirt-
/ be heard at both terminals of the Over-Sea Highway, as actual work has begun, and
st will be a welcoming host to thousands of motorists over this wonderful road.

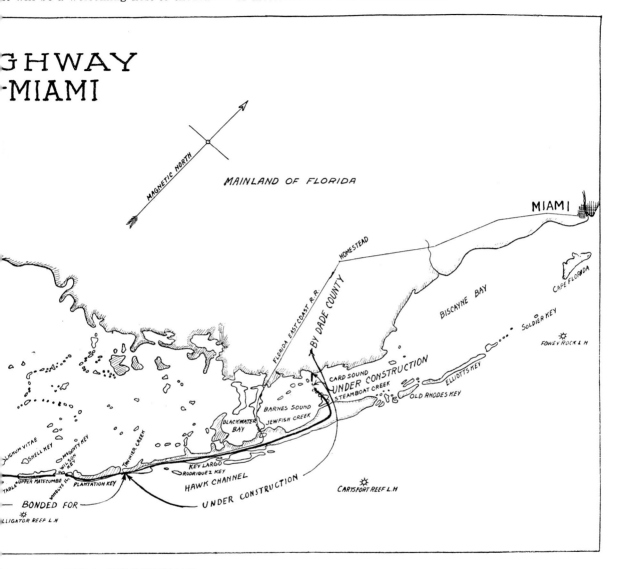

OVER-SEA HIGHWAY

already been commenced. The plan of construction agreed upon embraces the laying
le the road advances nearer and nearer to a central meeting point until it finally be-
ls have been sold for the purpose of carrying on this great undertaking and will furnish
ve and seven miles respectively. These gaps are water barriers that will have to be
:tion of such bridges; in the event that this proves unpracticable, ferries may be used,
may lunch in Key West—if he so desires.

telegram the following day for officials to be on the lookout for these two men "who supposedly left the city last evening."

THE FIRM of Jenner Bros. was awarded the contract to construct the highway from Key Largo to Upper Matecumbe. A crew is working *(above),* drilling holes for dynamite to blast open a borrow pit for fill. (Lowe)

REMINISCENT of the excavators used in constructing the railroad, a dredge lifts a bucket of fill onto a truck for building the Over-Sea Highway. (Lowe)

MACK'S PLACE on Key Largo was a welcome sight to motorists traveling the Over-Sea Highway. It was one of the first service stations to spring up along the highway. (Albury)

150-40

FOLLOWING THE CURVE of the railroad, the new highway takes shape near Tavernier. There were many complaints from motorists about washouts on the narrow 16-foot highway after a hurricane in 1926. It was widened a year later to 20 feet with two-foot marl-protected shoulders on each side. (HASF—Matlack)

YOU COULD MAIL a letter at the Rock Harbor Post Office, rent a motel room, view the beautiful Keys from a free observation tower, and arrange for fishing at this multi-purpose building on Key Largo. C. O. Garrett owned the building when this photograph was taken in the late 1920s. (Lowe)

ACROSS the newly constructed Over-Sea Highway from the Rock Harbor Post Office, C. O. Garrett had a restaurant where he advertised his modern, tower rooms and "cold drinks—all kinds." He enjoyed the distinction of having phone No. 1 in the Upper Keys. It was one of eight phones that worked on a system of long and short rings. (Lowe)

THE KEY LARGO BREEZE

Volume III—Number 10 | KEY LARGO, FLORIDA, WEDNESDAY, OCTOBER 26, 1927 | PRICE FIVE CENTS

COUNTY BUYS FERRIES FOR WATER GAPS

Construction Started October 17 by Jacksonville Firm

THREE 20-CAR BOATS TO DO 12-MILE SPEED

Auto Carriers for 40-Mile Water Stretch to Cost $120,000

The Monroe County commissioners on Oct. 15, sold time warrants to the value of $110,000, to Wright, Warlow and Company of Orlando, for the purpose of paying for three ferries for the deep-water gaps of the Oversea Highway.

Construction of these ferries was started in Jacksonville on the morning of Oct. 17, by the Gibbs Gas Engine Company. Each of the ferries will be fitted with two 100-horsepower Deisel engines, and when completed will be capable of making a speed of 12 miles an hour. The three ferries will cost $120,000.

Each ferry will have a capacity of 20 cars.

The action of the county commissioners in buying ferries was taken after investigation had been made into the feasibility of getting ferries operated on contract by private firms.

The ferries will be operated by the county over the 40-miles of water between Lower Matecumbe and No Name Key until such time as the state can build the bridges to connect the intervening sections of the highway. These bridges will cost about ten million dollars, engineers have estimated. The ferry charge contemplated is said to be five dollars per car each way.

The county is expected to advertise soon for bids for the construction of 14 miles of the Oversea Highway on the Key Vacas group of islands, between Lower Matecumbe and No Name Key. With completion of this stretch of the highway, the water haul will be shortened and the ferries will ply between Matecumbe and Key Vacas and Knights Key and No Name Key.

Lower Rates Florida's Big Prosperity Hope

Jacksonville, Fla., Oct. 26. (INS)—A guaranteed reduction in transportation and lodging rates is Florida's greatest hope for prosperity, according to State Hotel Commissioner Jerry W. Carter.

The guaranteed reduction in lodging rates is being offered by the state travel bureau, being operated under the asupices of the state hotel commission and Governor John W. Martin, through the sale of certificates good for a certain number of nights' hotel bills, entertainments, etc.

Florida Against Smith Because of Inheritance Tax Stand, Knight Says

Col. Peter O. Knight, banker and Democrat of Tampa in a recent interview in the New York Sun, expressed the conviction that Smith, if nominated for president could not carry Florida.

"One thing on which the Republicans and Democrats of Florida are all united is their opposition to the inheritance tax and their insistence upon its repeal,' Col. Knight said. "Especially do we object to the 80 per cent rebate provision of that law.

"Florida does not want the tax and does not need it: We have other means of raising revenue for state purposes. The chief reason for passing the inheritance tax law was to coerce states into adopting uniform laws on the subject. We hold that to be the province of the states and that the Federal government should not interfere in local taxation.

"At the hearing before the Ways and Means Committee when the revenue measure was under consideration, Mark Graves, the Tax Commissioner of New York, appeared and urged adoption of the 80 per cent rebate clause. His suggestion was adopted and enacted.

"The people of Florida hold that Gov. Smith was responsible for Graves' action and thereby largely responsible for this un-American inheritance tax. The last session of the Legislature in our state adopted unanimously a resolution denouncing the law and demanding that it be rescinded.

President Coolidge has denounced the act as legalized robbery. Gov. Smith has approved of the action of Graves. This overshadows all other issues in our state.

"Knowing this situation and how our people feel, it is my opinion that if Coolidge is nominated by the Republicans and Smith by the Democrats Florida is likely to vote for Coolidge. It would be voting for Coolidge, however, rather than for the Republican party. No other candidate the Republicans could name would have anything like the vote Coolidge would get.

"This tax situation is not all a Florida concern, although many have come to regard it as our battle. The Legislatures of twenty-two states have passed resolutions calling on Congress for repeal. A majority of the members of other Legislatures have signed petitions of the same purport. By the time the hearing on the measure is held by the Ways and Means Committee on November 6 to 8 forty states will have gone on record against the tax law.

"We hold that an inheritance tax is socialistic, if not communistic. Taxation should stop this side the grave. The present tax is not sound economically and is totally unfair. If there were an emergency and the government needed the money we would not rebel against even such an unfair proposition, but when the government does not need the money and the Federal government acts solely to coerce state government we do rebel.

"I am convinced that the South generally does not want to see Smith nominated. But if the Republicans name some other man than Coolidge and the Democrats do put up Smith, I think the governor will carry most of the southern states. There are some in the south who go so far as to say the nomination of Smith would wreck the party, but I do not agree with that."

Col. Knight is an optimist on Florida in particular and the South in general.

"The boom is all over and we are back to normal," he said. "And we are all right; conditions are very good. The period of deflation has passed and the substantial part of the boom period remains. The improvements are there and the same land and sunshine and natural resources.

"The condition of the banks tells the story. The deposits today are $600,000,000, as against $260,000,000 four years ago. Our winter business, meaning the tourist trade, will be considerably more than in 1924, the year before the boom."

REALTY MEN ARE FILING WRONG LICENSE FORMS

Chairman of State Commission Tells Requirements of New Law

Orlando, Fla., Oct. 26. (INS)—A large number of applications from registered real estate brokers and salesmen for renewal of registration certificates for the year beginning October 1 are being rejected due to the incomplete manner in which the forms are submitted, according to Walter W. Rose, chairman of the Florida Real Estate Commission.

Fees required under the new real estate brokers and salesman law and now in effect are $10 for an active broker, $5 for a salesman, and $1 for a non-active broker. In the case of a firm, either cor-

Orlando Makes Big Poultry Show Plans

Orlando, Fla., Oct. 26. (INS)—Extensive preparations were under way here today for the southern national poultry show to be staged in this city from December 7 to 10.

Earl W. Brown, of DeLand, prestry show, announced that the U. S. bureau of animal husbandry of the department of agriculture was sending a carload of exhibits for the show. Federal department of agriculture officials will attend their exhibit and give lectures.

HOLD SCHOOL FOR FARMERS

Fort Myers, Fla., Oct. 26. (INS)—The night school for farmers at Iona is reported to be drawing large numbers of prominent planters there each Tuesday night.

Similar schools will be held at Alva each Thursday night, according to county farm agent C. P. Wright, who is sponsoring the sessions.

BRIDGE TO KEYS MAY OPEN FOR TRAFFIC BY END OF WEEK IF WORK IS UNINTERRUPTED

Key Largo City Has New Publicity Organ

The Key Largo City News, a neatly arranged house organ of Key Largo City Properties, Inc., made its first appearance on October 8.

The only name in the masthead of the new publicity sheet, which is to be issued twice a month, is that of W. E. Lester, head of the industrial and commercial department of Key Largo City Properties, as publisher. John Chaffe, former assistant advertising manager for the Coral Gables Corporation, is editor, and Stephen Cochran Singleton, genial host for the development company at Key Largo City, is a contributing editor.

Billboard Advertising Eyesore, Says St. Pete

St. Petersburg, Fla., Oct. 26. (INS)—Keeping faith with the spirit of the recent state-wide campaign for ridding the highways of signs and other eye-sores, the board of governors of the local chamber of commerce has voted against a proposal to line state highways with billboards and signs advertising the city.

When the matter was brought up for discussion, Walter P. Fuller, Pinellas County chairman of the clean-up campaign and a member of the board of governors, registered a vigorous protest against the plan and called attention to the fact that the roads were already cluttered with billboards and signs which not only made this form of advertising ineffectual, but also marred the beauty of the state along the main arteries of travel.

OIL DRILLING IS WATCHED BY MANY SUNDAY

150 Persons See "Bit" Hoisted From Hole 597 Feet Deep

The oil well drill operated by J. M. Russell a mile and a half south of Florida City on the Key Largo Road had penetrated to 597 feet Sunday afternoon when the drill was withdrawn from the hole while approximately one hundred fifty persons looked on.

The drilling, financed by a stock company headed by Russell, who says the limestone structure of the earth at this spot has convinced him that oil is there, was started a week ago. The depth of the oil well was easily checked Sunday by the spectators who watched the crew of the drill hoist out seven 80-foot sections of four-inch pipe and several shorter lengths. Screwed into the bottom end of the last

100 Feet of Decking to Complete Mainland-Key Largo Structure

BEGIN WORK IN 30 DAYS ON APPROACH

4-Mile Road From Bridge to Key Largo to Be Entirely Rebuilt

Delayed by lack of material and later by lack of men, reconstruction work on the bridge connecting Key Largo and the Overs[illegible] Highway with the mainland is [illegible]ally nearing completion, [illegible] there is no let up in the w[illegible] bridge may be opened to tra[illegible] the end of this week, according [illegible] W. R. Milner, resident engineer of Monroe County.

All that remains to be done is laying of about one hundred feet of decking (flooring), and the erection of several hundred feet of railing. The bridge, which is 16 feet wide, has a 4-inch by 6-inch wheel guard and a strong hand rail on each edge of it, securely bolted to the pile heafs. The wheel guards are timbers which will turn the wheels of an automobile back toward the middle of the bridge if the wheels come in contact with them. The S. J. Groves & Sons Company firm is doing the bridge reconstruction.

Scores of persons from Miami, Homestead and other parts of Dade County fished from the uncompleted bridge Sunday. Next Sunday it is expected that they can motor across to Key Largo.

Reconstruction of the Oversea Highway from the bridge to the point where it turns into Key Largo will be started in 30 days by Jenner Bros., whose roadwork, covering the sections of the Oversea Highway from Key Largo to Upper Mattacumbe was accepted by the county recently after an inspection by a committee of county commissioners.

The bridge approach road, nearly four miles in length, will be completely rebuilt in a manner that will give protection from damage by high water in the future, Mr. Milner said. It is now only 16 feet wide, but when reconstructed it will be 20 feet wide and have a two-foot marl protective shoulder on each side. In its present state, the road has been a menace to motor travel because of the wash-outs and ruts resulting from last year's hurricane.

Football Game Arranged By Tampa in 4 Minutes

Tampa, Fla., Oct. 26. (INS)—One of the most unique and fastest scheduling of a football game in history took place here when the Tampa post of the American Legion closed with the marine navy base at Key West for a tilt between

THE CARD SOUND BRIDGE linking the mainland to Key Largo neared completion when this issue of *The Key Largo Breeze* came out October 26, 1927. Edited by Key Wester Benjamin E. Archer who had become a newspaper publisher in Homestead, the land boom paper also announced the Monroe County Commission's order for three ferries to carry vehicles over the highway's watergaps. Ferries initially operated from Lower Matecumbe to No Name Key—a distance of 40 miles. (Knowles)

VIEW FROM atop the Moser Channel swing bridge looks southward over the Seven Mile Bridge. Bridges were designed for higher speeds but trains crossed cautiously at 15 miles per hour. Passengers could settle back and enjoy a half hour trip across the Seven Mile Bridge. (FSU)

IT'S HARD to imagine what sounds except that of a train whistling on the Seven-Mile Bridge would interrupt the quietness of this one room schoolhouse on Pigeon Key. The sign "School—Quiet Zone" is posted, nonetheless, at this public school photographed in December, 1926. (HASF—Matlack)

THE "HAVANA SPECIAL," the Miami express, crosses Long Key Viaduct. The train stopped for this "posed" shot taken by Harry Wolfe, official photographer of the Florida East Coast Railway. Although the company advertised a four and a half hour trip from Key West to Miami, the train usually arrived about two hours late. (Perez)

AS A PROMOTIONAL STUNT, a new LaSalle was driven over the railroad ties from Miami to Key West in December, 1927. A crowd gathers at Long Key Fishing Camp *(left)* to see the drivers off. The LaSalle bounces along the Long Key Viaduct *(below)*. While crossing bridges, the drivers wore life jackets. (HASF—Matlack)

72

THE PROMOTIONAL STUNT was recorded by cameramen on this railroad car traveling behind the LaSalle. The gasoline-powered railroad car also carried mechanics and spare parts. (HASF—Matlack)

R. C. PERKY had this bat tower constructed on Perky (now Sugarloaf Key). Mr. Perky ran a fishing lodge, but his guests were plagued by swarms of mosquitoes. Hearing about bats gobbling up mosquitoes in San Antonio, Texas, Perky got the plans for the tower and purchased a smelly bait to attract bats. The scheme never worked, but the tower stands today—a monument to Perky, who dedicated it "to good health March 15, 1929." (Anderson)

A COW strolls about Pigeon Key. The small island beneath the Seven-Mile Bridge had a population of mostly railroad families. (HASF—Matlack)

73

THE FIRST CAR traveled the newly completed Over-Sea Highway on January 25, 1928. This bridge between Stock Island and Boca Chica was one of 30 in the project. (LC)

Facing Page: WHEN THE LAND BOOM fizzled out on George Merrick, developer of Coral Gables, he retreated to the Keys in the early 1930s. The visionary Merrick conceived of a development on Islamorada. The Caribbee Colony was located next to what is today's Lindback's Siesta Motel. (HASF—Matlack)

The Florida Keys from 1930 to 1940

SHORT ON POPULATION, but rich in local color, Tavernier made the CBS airwaves every Wednesday night in 1931, as the setting for the imaginary "Junction City." The weekly program, originating from station WQAM in Miami, was a brainchild of Leonard Cox who, with his wife, Lila Vaughn Cox, had a winter home in Tavernier and an immense curiosity about the community and its few residents. Cox, who had been a writer for the Fred Allen Show, turned his gleanings of fact and fiction into one-hour episodes aired under the Junction City title. A Tavernier native and regular on the show was Capt. Eugene Lowe (in tuxedo upper left) who played the role of Attorney Curry. Other Tavernier residents were frequently enlisted for bit parts, one being Capt. Lowe's wife, Myrtle. She is directly behind the seated man. (Lowe)

LEFT OVER from railroad construction days, this building served as the Marathon Post Office in the late 1920s and early 1930s. Three railroad cross-ties were used to make the walkway in front of the building. (Anderson)

A BEVY OF YOUNG WOMEN enjoy sunning and relaxing after a day of fishing at the Key Largo Anglers Club in January 1932. Photographer G. W. Romer brought the models down from Miami to shoot a feature on fashions. (MDPL—Romer)

78 LOCOMOTIVE No. 435 slowly crosses the Seven-Mile Bridge. The photograph was taken by railroad photographer Harry Wolfe as the train approached Pigeon Key. (Fontis)

THE TRAIN stops at Long Key Fishing Camp. The camp attracted many prominent visitors—including Herbert Hoover and Franklin D. Roosevelt in the early 1930s. (Anderson)

Telegraph Calls	Telegraph Stations	Distance from Jacksonville	TIME TABLE No. 7 Feb. 17, 1932 FIFTH DISTRICT STATIONS	Passing Tracks Capacity 42 Ft. Cars	Other Tracks Capacity 42 Ft. Cars	FIRST CLASS 76 Havana Special Daily	SECOND CLASS	THIRD CLASS 230 Local Freight Daily
DI	X N	365.6	†MIAMI South End Double Track		1032	S 9.30		
CG	X D	370.9	†COCONUT GROVE 2.9	110	198	S 9.14		
	X	373.8	*SOUTH MIAMI 2.6	76	64	S 9.09		
	X	376.3	KENDAL 3.2	100	126	9.05		2.40
	X	379.5	*KEYS	69		F 9.00		2.05
FR	X D	381.6	†PERRINE 4.2	79	65	S 8.56		1.50
GS	X D	385.8	†GOULDS...w	91	129	S 8.46		1.22
PN	X	387.7	*PRINCETON 1.9	48	9	S 8.41		1.08
	Y	389.4	*NARANJA 1.7	107	50	S 8.36		12.57
	X	391.5	*MODELLO 2.1	72	22	F 8.31		12.45
ID	X D	393.9	†HOMESTEAD..w 2.4	35	192	S 8.26		12.30 11.40
D	X D	395.6	*FLORIDA CITY 1.7	76	50	F 8.16		11.22
	X	401.6	*WOODDALL 6.0	67		8.09		11.05
	X	408.3	*GLADES...w 6.7		5	F 8.00		10.46
	X	412.4	*CROSS KEY 4.9	73		7.54		10.35
	X	417.3	*KEYLARGO	64	10	F 7.47		10.20
	X	424.4	*ROCKHARBOR 6.6	75		F 7.35		10.00
	X	431.0	*TAVERNIER 9.1	64	27	F 7.26		9.41
MA	X D	440.1	*ISLAMORADA..w	46	17	F 7.12		9.14 [71]
	X	447.6	*CREVALLO 7.5	64		7.00		8.49
	X	455.1	*ROSSMORE 2.2	50		6.49		8.32 [H]
	X	457.3	*LONG KEY 7.1	39	13	F 6.44		8.15
	X	464.4	*GRASSY 6.5	46		6.34		7.55
	X	470.9	*VACA 3.2	59		6.23		7.37
KY	X D	474.1	†MARATHON..w 3.9	48	144	S 6.18		7.29
	X	478.0	*PIGEON KEY 7.1			F 6.04		
	X	485.1	*BAHIA HONDA 6.8	69		5.51		7.01
	X	491.9	*BIG PINE 8.0	69	5	F 5.42		6.44
	X	499.9	*CUDJOE...w 6.1	76	9	5.30		6.25
	X	506.0	*PERKY 6.2	51		F 5.21		6.11
	X	512.2	*BIG COPPITT 6.3	51		5.14		5.56
	X	518.5	*STOCK ISLAND 3.5	75		5.07		5.42
KD	X D	522.0	†KEY WEST..w		782	5.00		5.30
						76		230

THIS TIMETABLE of February 17, 1932, was used by employees of the Florida East Coast Railway and notes such information as the distance from Jacksonville and the location of telegraph stations. "Vaca," just three miles north of Marathon, never had an agent. It was built at the insistence of residents who refused to give the railroad the right to cross their land unless Flagler made it a flag stop. (Fontis)

THE TAVERN TEA ROOM at Tavernier shortly after it was completed in 1932. Harry Harris,
later to become Monroe County Commissioner
and Mayor, operated a restaurant from the
renovated building in the late 1930s. (Byrum)

WOODBURN'S GENERAL STORE, located
on the north side of the railroad tracks in
Marathon in the early 1930s. Although the store
had a U. S. mail slot to the right of the entrance, it
has not been determined if it actually was a post
office or simply a mail drop. (Anderson)

RED MANGROVES—the bushes that make islands. Mangrove roots collect debris and eventually clumps of mushy land
begin to form. (Sprunt)

THE PIRATES COVE FISHING CAMP at Sugarloaf Key became a mecca for fishermen and vacationers like its counterpart on Long Key. C. Irving Wright, a wealthy New England shoe manufacturer, had the camp built in 1929 and 1930. The old highway is shown passing through the camp as it heads toward the wooden bridge that parallels the railroad bridge over to Cudjoe Key. (MDPL—Romer)

WRIGHT PUBLICIZED Pirates Cove as a former haunt of pirates, suggesting even Blackbeard himself used it. When it opened in 1930, the camp had accommodations for 30 persons who stayed in cottages like these. (MDPL—Romer)

GUESTS ate in the comfort of a screened porch at the lodge. The lodge kitchen had a 12-burner gas range and a huge refrigerator which held a variety of food to please the well-heeled guests. (MDPL—Romer)

WHILE THE MEN FISHED, women could enjoy a protected salt water pool, deck tennis, and bridge. "Pirates Cove is the only fishing resort where women can enjoy comfort and luxury while their husbands bring in the fish," a writer once stated. The camp was virtually destroyed in the 1948 hurricane. (MDPL—Romer)

81

WHILE PROTECTING BIRDS and their nesting areas from poachers, Audubon Society wardens ran into this crocodile in the Upper Keys. *(below)*. Warden Ed Moore confiscated these bird traps *(left)* from an illicit bird dealer in Key West. Trapping wild birds on the Keys was once a lucrative business. Moore's sons, Peter and Ed Jr., are shown with the traps. (Sprunt)

THE HIGHWAY GOSPEL HALL was built on Upper Matecumbe in 1930s by lay preacher and businessman Copeland Johnson of Key West. The church was destroyed in the 1935 hurricane which also claimed the lives of Johnson and his wife who had visited the church that Labor Day weekend. (MCPL)

WAREHOUSES and home with a down-spout to funnel water into a wooden tank were located between the Over-Sea Highway and the railroad tracks in Tavernier in the early 1930s. (Byrum)

THE TAVERNIER Railroad Station (top right), was further to the north, and across the tracks stood a warehouse where limes and other crops were stored before being shipped out. (Byrum)

TAKEN from a water tower built by H. S. (Mr. Mac) McKenzie to supply his businesses and nearby homes, this photograph is looking south. Building in the center is Keys Utility Co. Florida Power and Light Co. had taken over the operation at this time. (Byrum)

One for All---All for One
THE KEY VETERAN NEWS
PUBLISHED WEEKLY BY THE VETERANS WORK PROGRAM CAMPS IN FLORIDA ON THE KEYS

VOLUME ONE | ISLAMORADA, FLORIDA, SATURDAY, JULY 20, 1935. | NUMBER SEVENTEEN.

NEARBY KEYS IN NATIONAL TROPICS PARK

Area of 1,300,000 Acres Includes Cape Sable and Royal Palm Park

SCIENTIST TELLS OF EXPLORATION IN 1903

First Roosevelt Tried to Make U. S. Preserve of Paradise Key

Although the idea of creating a tropical national park on the southern tip of Florida was put forward in 1903, it was not until last year that an enabling measure was passed by Congress to permit its accomplishment. It will be known as the Everglades National Park, as it will embrace mostly everglade country.

Rare tropical birds and a great amount of game exist in the area because it has been almost impenetrable on account of the dense tropical growth and undrained lands. It is the only place in the United States where Royal Palm trees have been found growing wild—many of them 100 feet high.

The area is located in Dade, Monroe, and Collier Counties, and is conceded to be the most truly tropical portion of the mainland of the United States. It includes Cape Sable, the southern extremity of the Florida peninsula and the most southern point of the mainland of the United States, and extends from that cape some 45 miles northerly along the Gulf of Mexico and some 50 miles easterly along the Bay of Florida.

Northwardly the park area as planned extends about 10 or 15 miles north of the Tamiami Trail. Altogether there is a total of about 2,000 square miles involved, or nearly 1,300,000 acres.

The southern boundary of the (Continued on Page Five)

WELAKA PICNIC REVEALS TRACK STARS IN CAMP 7

Long Awaited Crescent Beach Outing Huge Success

By ABE KLYMAN

One hundred and fifty members of Camp Seven, Welaka, were transported to Crescent Beach Saturday, the 13th, for a full day of recreation and sport.

The men arrived in a carefree mood, prepared to enjoy to the utmost the many good things in store for them. Tents and troop kitchens had been erected on the eve of the big day. Fifty cases of beer were on hand, supplemented by many cases of soda pop, cigars and cigarettes—plenty for all.

The men arrived in the late forenoon to find everything in readi-

1918 -- 1935
STILL GUNNING---BUT DIFFERENT GAME

Cawthon Joins Staff Of Key Veteran News

Wilbur B. Cawthon of Camp Three has taken over the vacancy on the News staff formerly filled by J. B. Barker.

Cawthon saw two years overseas service with the Motor Transport Corps and he completed his regular army duty as instructor at the motor

OPPORTUNITY

Is there an ornamental iron worker, cabinet maker or potter among the veteran personnel? If so, he is asked to get in touch with J. Marquette Phillips, 432 41st street, Miami Beach, or call at the News office. This may mean your break.

All Stars to Play Ball
At South Miami Sunday

Condition of Kubiak Reported Favorable

Reports from the Jackson Memorial hospital at Miami describe the condition of John Kubiak, who was injured in a motor accident on July Fourth, as very favorable.

Kubiak has made excellent progress toward recovery and hospital authorities have hopes of restoring

FIND PLANT THAT ROUTS MOSQUITOES

Discovered on Bamboo Key Where Insect Never Appears

IS LIKE CITRONELLA GRASS, PEST CHASER

Key West Engineer Plants Results of Search on Golf Course

A. C. Tanner, sanitary engineer in Key West, is of the opinion he may have discovered the reason there are no mosquitoes found on Bamboo Key and sections of other keys in these waters.

About one week ago, with Fernando Camus and others of the sanitary department, Mr. Tanner was cruising among the keys with an idea of finding out why with hordes of mosquitoes in the vicinity of Bamboo it was possible to explore that key from one end to the other, in a nude state, and never be stung.

He discovered a growth, which he at first thought was citronella grass, and ropogon nardus, native to southern Asia, which yields citronella oil, used to drive away mosquitoes.

Closer investigation showed that it was not a grass but an epiphyte, one of the many parasite growths found in tropical regions, and all of the specimens secured were clinging with small tendrils to parsley, which is luxuriantly growing on Bamboo Key.

It was also shown that two other places, one at Channel Key and another at Marquesas, were free from mosquitoes, and at both of these places this epiphyte was found in abundance.

Mr. Tanner brought some of the growth to Key West, and is to experiment with it at the golf course. If he is successful in his experiment, he is satisfied the golf course will be free of mosquitoes at all seasons.
—Key West Citizen.

GAME FORFEITED BY KEY WEST IN SEVENTH INNING

Score 6-5 for Island City When Visiting Catcher Is Injured

Last Sunday the fans were deprived of witnessing the finish of an exciting ball game when Rodriguez, catcher for the Key West nine, was injured as Voyles slid into home plate in the last half of the seventh inning. No other receiver being available, the Key West manager pulled his team off the field and according to the rules forfeited the game to the Vets, 9 to 0.

The accident was unavoidable and occurs every now and then in close plays on the diamond. Voyles, the

UNDER THE Federal Works Relief program, World War I veterans were stationed in camps on the Keys and given jobs in mosquito control and building a bridge from Lower Matecumbe to Long Key. *The Key Veteran News* was a weekly newspaper whose first issue of March 30, 1935, stated that the paper would show that veterans "are not the flotsam and jetsam and human derelicts that the stereotyped sob writers would have you believe . . ." (Archer)

Associated Press Day Wire Service.
For 55 Years Devoted to the Best Interests of Key West

The Key West Citizen

Key West, Florida, has the most equable weather in the country; with an average range of only 14° Fahrenheit

VOLUME LVI. No. 211. KEY WEST, FLORIDA, THURSDAY, SEPTEMBER 5, 1935. PRICE FIVE CENTS

DEATH TOLL ON FLORIDA KEYS MOUNTS

MANY PERSONS ALSO INJURED

Great Destruction From Hurricane At Tavernier, Matecumbe And Several Other Points

With each passing hour details of the terrible hurricane and its ravages on the Keys become more heart-breaking and terrifying.

In another column in The Citizen appears a list of persons saved, dead and missing and other information relative to this great catastrophe. But this does not by no means convey an idea of the vast property destruction and loss of life caused by the raging of the elements.

From various sources there come many stories of death and destruction. Some of these have been verified and others have been proven unfounded. In times like these, it is said, it is well for readers to heed only those reports which come from authentic sources and pay no attention to the hundreds of rumors which are heard on every hand.

A summary of news items received by The Citizen during the past 24 hours is given herwith:

In a radio message received by the sheriff's office, B. M. Duncan advises that "Lewis and John are missing. Rest of the ferry crew safe. Also missing are Joe Lowe, Clarence Jones and Neff and son. Arrived at camp walking from Marathon. Continuing North. Extensive damage done at Lower Matecumbe with Camp 3 practically wiped out. All bridge equipment still here but damaged."

Attorney and Mrs. Raymond Lord and daughter, Joan Ray and Eugene Sands, who were at Marathon, guests of Mr. and Mrs. W. A. Parrish and family for several days, returned last night on the train from Marathon. Miss Lou Roberts was also a returning passenger.

Mr. Sands told The Citiztn that the Parrish home and fish house were totally destroyed and he, his family and guests were forced to take refuge at the Sombrero Fishing Lodge, managed by Ted Harvey.

After the storm a survey was made of the island and four negroes were declared missing. One injured negro was brought to Key West for treatment.

This morning a telegram was received from Mr. Parrish by Chief Deputy Bernard Waite, advising that Ferris Farrington had been found dead in his boat this morning. The body arrived on the afternoon train from Marathon.

Another telegram was received at the sheriff's office from Sheriff K. O. Thompson in which it is advised "condition much worse than I anticipated. Will be back Friday. Have been unable to reach either Tavernier or Islamorada.

Damage to Alligator Reef lighthouse will total about $10,000,

(Continued on Page Four)

JOHNSON TELLS OF DISASTER IN MATECUMBE AREA

MADE TRIP BY PLANE AND SURVEYED CONDITIONS; DESCRIBES IT AS SCENE OF GREAT DESOLATION

"The Matecumbe area and surrounding territory presented the worst scene of destruction and desolation which I have ever seen," said Fred Johnson, superintendent at Perky, Fla., who arrived there yesterday from Miami.

Mr. Johnson made the trip by plane to Key West and after a short time with his family returned to his headquarters where he was contacted over long distance phone by The Citizen.

Matecumbe is flat. Nothing left standing in all that section except one building at Tavernier and of the many thousands of coconut trees only a few are left.

Long Key is another scene which is evidence of the terrific forces of wind and waves, said Mr. Johnson. Ravages of the elements seen on every hand.

Asked how many dead persons he had seen he said that a conservative estimate would be about 10 but he did not have any idea of the loss of life among the veterans especially those who were on the train which was sent from Miami to take them to Hollywood.

He said that about 10 cars were washed from the tracks and several of the cars look to be about 400 feet from the right-of-way. It was there he believed that the greatest loss of life will be recorded.

Mr. Johnson said that there were approximately 30 miles of track washed out altogether. That while the concrete viaducts were standing and apparently uninjured there were many places on them where the ties and tracks had completely disappeared. In other places the tracks were there but warped and twisted so as to be useless. At Key Vacas several miles of track and fill seemed to have disappeared.

Other terrible evidences of the fury of the winds were a great number of automobiles at different points on the keys which were apparently smashed and twisted out of shape.

"I have heard of the destruction wrought by storms and winds, and have seen the ravages of the elements here in Key West when I was much younger, but never have I imagined that such a beautiful and prosperous section of the country could be transformed into such a terrible picture of devastation, suffering and woe, as that part of the Florida Keys over which I passed this morning," said Mr. Johnson.

Mr. Johnson concluded by saying that the Perky property was not at all affected by either wind or water.

ADVISORY

Storm, Information

Southeast storm warnings continued at Savannah, Ga., to New Bern, N. C. Tropical disturbance, decreased in intensity, is central over southeastern Georgia moving northeastward with increasing rapidity. Will cause southeast gales on the coast and strong shifting winds near center' this afternoon and tonight diminishing south of Wilmington tonight.

OFFICIALS WILL TAKE UP FRESH WATER QUESTION

ENGINEERING UNIT OF FERA ORGANIZATION LEAVE FOR TALLAHASSEE FOR CONSULTATION

John A. C. Bogart, assistant to H. S. Riddle, consultant engineer, FERA in Florida, and F. H. McKinley, attached to the PWA engineering branch in Key West, left yesterday afternoon on the Steamship Cuba, for Tampa enroute to Tallahassee for a consultation relative to water pipe lines for Key West.

At meetings held the early part of the week this matter was settled with the city council which held two meetings for the purpose of passing resolutions relative to the matter, the gist of the resolutions being as follows:

Mayor Wm. H. Malone was authorized to file with the federal authorities an application for a loan and grant to aid in financing construction of water pipe lines from Key West to the source of supply.

H. S. Riddle, consultant engineer with FERA and John A. C. Bogart, sanitary engineer, are directed to furnish such information as the United States government through the FERA may reasonably request in connection with the application.

City Attorney J. Lancelot Lester was authorized to furnish such legal information to the Federal Emergency Relief Administration of Public Works necessary to support the application and Willard M. Albury, city auditor, was authorized to furnish any financial information required and H. S. Riddle and John A. C. Bogart will furnish engineering information needed in support of the application.

COMPILING LIST OF KEY GROUPS

FERA WILL MAKE KNOWN PERSONS LOST OR INJURED

A list of all known residents on the Florida Keys was being prepared this morning by the Key West Administration in an effort to ascertain as soon as possible the names of persons injured or lost through the hurricane Monday night and Tuesday.

Through telephone communication with No Name Key the Administration hopes to have the names of as many as possible compiled. Boats in the rescue party which left here yesterday were returning this morning to No Name Key from the stricken area and from persons aboard them it was hoped authentic information could be obtained.

Compilation of the list of names of persons known to be residing on the Keys is being made by F. Townsend Morgan. All registered citizens there are being ascertained from the court house records, and in addition a compilation of the names of all relief clients is being furnished by Mrs. Nina Ryder Johnson.

The complete list will be available at the Administration offices, J. Gerry Curtis, acting administrator, said.

CHURCH SUPPER IS POSTPONED

Announcement has been made by St. Paul's Choir Guild that the Parish Entertainment and Supper which was to be held on Tuesday, September 10, has been indefinitely postponed on account of the great anxiety and sadness in the city following the great disaster on the keys from the tropical storm.

THREE APPLY FOR POSITION OF PROBATION OFFICER; COUNTY BOARD HEARS OTHER MATTERS LAST NIGHT

Applications for the position of probation officer of Monroe county from William T. H. Boll, J. Carlyle Roberts and Richard H. Sawyer were read last night at the meeting of the county commissioners, and on motion they were referred to Governor Sholtz, without recommendation.

Present at the meeting were Chairman Carl Bervaldi, Commissioners Wm. R. Porter, Braxton B. Warren and Nathan Niles; Clerk Ross C. Sawyer and Chief Deputy Bernard Waite. Judge D. A. McDougal, of Washington, was also present.

Judge McDougal addressed the board relative to his immense holdings in the county, and expressed his appreciation at the fair and equitable decision regarding tax reductions which were tentatively agreed upon at a meeting of the tax adjustment board, several weeks ago.

To Arrange Settlement

The judge said he was to leave Key West in a few days for Oklahoma, there to make arrangements for the settlement of the delinquent taxes due the county on the land.

Relative to the applications for probation officer it was the sense of the board that with the applications there be sent to the governor an opinion of the board members that the appointment of a probation officer at this time is without justification in consideration of the financial condition of the county. The job of probation officer was characterized by Mr. Porter as a sinecure.

Report of Sheriff K. O. Thompson of deposits in the First National Bank for August showed a total of $102.66.

Tax Collector Frank H. Ladd reported deposits of $749.05 during the month of August to the different funds, distributed as follows:

General Revenue, $128.18;
Fine and Forfeiture, $39.63;
Outstanding Indebtedness Fund, $184.94;
Special Advertising, $13.21;
Special Bond and Interest, $26.42;
Road Fund, $26.42;
General School, $132.10;
Special School Bond and Interest, $66.05;
Special School Tax District Number 1, $132.10.

In connection with the above the collector's report shows as remitted to State Treasurer W. V. Knott, as county treasurer ex-officio, $458.12, less commissions of $8.98, net $449.14.

County Judge Hugh Gunn's report showed license issued to other than merchants with total revenue of $40—$25 to the state and $15 to the county.

Clerk Sawyer reported $4,231.59, cash and bonds, on redemption or purchases of tax certificates during the month of August.

Discuss Liquor Licenses

Liquor applications, which were received at the last regular meeting of the board were discussed. Those of Saunders Wholesale Grocery, Charles I. and Lumley Park, Raul Vasquez, Albino Morales and Aquilino Lopez, were approved by the board.

Applications of Joseph S. Russell, "Sloppy Joe's," and George Low, Driftwood Hotel at Tavernier, were held over for the recessed meeting to be held September 11.

Liquor license applications received last night were from Oscar Solano, Jose Lopez, Georgina Hernandez Sosin, Jose Sanchez and Juan Carbonell. These will be passed on at the next meeting of the board.

Resolutions were adopted requesting permission from State Treasurer Knott to transfer from the Indebtedness Fund $1,100 to the General Revenue Fund and $700 to the Fine and Forfeiture Fund, in order to make a payroll for employes in those branches of the county's government.

A number of bond offerings which were received following the advertisement in The Citizen calling for bids, were unanimously refused.

In a communication from the governor's office attention was called to the proposed fund for generally advertising the state, to be designated as the All Florida Advertising Fund, with a proposed 10 cents per capita appropriation, which the county had tentatively agreed upon.

It was the opinion of the board that the governor's office be advised that in view of the great catastrophe which has visited Monroe county, especially on the keys, the resources of the county will be greatly overtaxed to render necessary assistance to the stricken families in the district.

Following the regular meeting the board met as the delinquent tax adjustment board, discussed a number of adjustments as prepared by Clerk Sawyer, and approved them, after which a recess was ordered.

CUBA ARRIVES SAFE AT TAMPA

CAPTAIN HARRINGTON SENDS WIRE ANNOUNCING ARRIVAL OF SHIP

Mrs. C. D. Harrington, wife of Captain Harrington of the P. and O. S. S. Cuba, this afternoon received a telegram from the captain advising that the vessel reached Tampa in safety this morning.

As there were a number of Key Westers, and friends who were visiting in Key West, there was a feeling of uneasiness prevalent here as to the safety of the voyagers. This news will relieve their anxiety.

E. WHITMARSH DIES IN TAMPA

Thomas F. Whitmarsh, of Olivia street, received a wire today advising him of the death of his brother, Ernest Whitmarsh, in Tampa.

No other information was contained in the telegram.

TAKING INJURED ONES TO MIAMI

WILL BE GIVEN TREATMENT THERE, ACCORDING TO ANNOUNCEMENT

Injured persons on the Keys are being taken into Miami for treatment, according to a radio message sent by M. E. Gilfond to Dr. E. H. Carnes this morning.

Three doctors who were taken by Mr. Gilfond to Matecumbe, where he is located now, have left for Miami to aid in administering to the injured, the message said. In a later radiogram, medical supplies, including rubber gloves, disinfectant, and similar commodities were requested by the administrator.

Ten boats have been placed at the disposal of the Administration for carrying medical and food supplies to Matecumbe from No Name Key.

This morning, no one who went to Matecumbe from No Name Key had returned to No name, so that definite information, verified by telephone conversation was still lacking.

CARETAKER AT LONG KEY GIVES STORM ACCOUNT

VIVID DESCRIPTION FURNISHED BY J. E. DUANE, WHO WAS STATIONED AT KEY'S FISHING CAMP

A vivid eyewitness account of the terrible and disastrous hurricane of Monday is being told by J. E. Duane, caretaker of Long Key Fishing Camp, who miraculously escaped with his life after going through the camp situated at that place and owned and operated by the Florida East Coast Hotel Company.

Besides Mr. Duane there were nineteen other persons at the camp but all have lived to tell the tale of suffering which they will long remember. The 19 persons included Fran Thorn, carpenter; Paul Richardson and Oscar Collins, member of a repair crew; a section foreman, Mr. Rousch, his wife and four small children; eight section hands and two women, the last ten being colored.

The section foreman and family arrived at Long Key the morning of the storm from further up the line from which point he had been transferred to Long Key.

Began At 4 O'Clock

While in the buildings the men report that they had to hold the four little children over their heads to keep them from drowning. They were breast deep in water for over a half hour.

According to Mr. Duane the storm began of hurricane intensity about 4 p. m. on Monday and the wind increased hourly from a northerly direction while the barometer fell at the rate of .01 inch every five minutes. By six o'clock the building began to give way under the lash of the storm and the water rose on the northly side of the island and by 9:30 p. m. was 18 or 20 feet deep on the north side of the island. In fact the water was nearly up as high as the railroad tracks and was being held back by the embankment.

Around 9:20 p. m. the center or eye of the storm passed over at which time the stars were visible over the island and to the eastward for a distance of four or five miles.

Blew 175 to 200 Miles An Hour

The seas were mountainous and the barometer was very low. About 10:10 p. m. the wind came from the opposite direction before the lull and was carried along by a gale estimatel at 175 to 200 miles an hour. The water rose rapidly over the southerly side of the island. Mr. Duane and a companion were on the porch of a building made a dash for another building about 60 feet distant but before they reached the door they were inundated to a depth waist high.

They succeeded in gaining entrance to the building where the other people had gone for safety but by this time the water had risen enough that the building of Lady Ashley, whose home became the refuge, was afloat and beginning to break up. Mr. Duane was trapped in the hallway and in a moment was precipitated through an opening into the sea. He fought his way through the water and grasped the top of a coconut tree and clung to the broken fronds.

Knocked Unconscious

In a few minutes he noticed the building containing the people floating out to sea but lost consciousness when struck on the back of the head by floating debris. When he became conscious he saw that he was lodged in the tree 20 feet above the ground and the building with the people had been carried back on shore by the wind when it had abruptly shifted and came from a southerly direction.

The wind was still blowing at a hurricane velocity but soon

(Continued on Page Four)

Death List From Storm May Reach One Thousand

EVERYONE AS FAR SOUTH AS CARABEE COLONY HAS BEEN MOVED OUT; DEAD ARE NOW BEING CARRIED AWAY; HORRIBLE SCENE REPORTED ALL ALONG STORM-STRICKEN AREA

(Copyrighted—Associated Press)

MIAMI, Sept. 5.—Swiftly and uneventfully the last group of passengers was removed from the stranded and battered Liner Dixie today while relief workers hurried to take all injured persons on the hurricane-stricken Florida Keys to Miami and began to gather bodies of the dead.

One hundred and forty-three passengers were left on the Dixie last night when higher winds halted transfer in the rescue. All were removed from the liner, which was thrown aground Monday night by the raging hurricane, within three hours today.

NO ACCURATE CHECK AS YET

In the meanwhile an accurate check of fatalities on the barren Keys was impossible with estimates of rescue workers ranging from 200 to 500.

W. P. Mooty, of Miami, personal representative of Governor Sholtz in the hurricane area, advised the chief executive the deaths from the storm "may reach one thousand."

"Words cannot describe the horrible disaster," Mr. Mooty said in a telegram to the governor. "Everyone as far south as Carabee Colony has been moved out, the injured first. They are now moving the dead. Fifty so far. Rebuilding bridges to cross Snake Creek."

It was Snake Creek, then a raging torrent, that prevented immediate penetrating of the Keys Tuesday to learn the fate of war veterans quartered at three camps.

The tropical disturbance, its hurricane winds lost on moving inland near Cedar Keys yesterday, was centered in south central Georgia today headed at a quickening pace for the Atlantic Ocean.

Fifty-one bodies, "very few identified," lay in the morgue here. All were bodies of men, except one woman and two girls. Leonard K. Thompson, in charge of local Red Cross relief, said "that's a matter for the government to decide," when asked today concerning reports that bodies of storm victims would be cremated on the Keys.

GOVERNOR MAKES TOUR OF KEYS

Governor Sholtz left Tallahassee early today by automobile to tour the Keys.

Fears were felt at Cedar Keys, probably the worst damaged city on the west coast, for lives of four fishermen who set out in two small craft Tuesday. They had not returned today, hours after the howling hurricane had struck at the Cedar Keys area with 100-mile winds.

In one boat were Vinson McCloud and Jim McCloud and Reddy Davis and Ray Campbell were in the other.

Rescued passengers off the Dixie were brought here and told of singing merry tunes as the destruction appeared inevitable as mountainous waves smashed the vessel harder and harder upon the coral sand bottom. Calmly they told of bravery of the crew.

Bewildered survivors of the Keys disaster told of the night of horror as howling winds and thundering waves battered their fellows to death. Seventy men of Camp Number Three on Lower Matecumbe Key, virtually the only survivors there, clung through the night to a tank car filled with water.

NO ONE KNEW how many people had died when the Labor Day hurricane of September 2, 1935 hit the Florida Keys. Communications were knocked out and Key Westers, having enjoyed a calm and sunny Monday, could hardly believe the radio reports. (Knowles—*The Key West Citizen*)

A RELIEF TRAIN was sent to pick up veterans trapped in the path of the hurricane. It arrived at Snake Creek late that Monday afternoon after experiencing many delays—including a decision at Homestead to turn the train around and go backwards down the Keys. After taking on the veterans and others at Snake Creek, the train made it to Islamorada, but a tidal wave pushed by 200 mile per hour winds knocked the train off the tracks. The eye of the hurricane passed over Islamorada that night. The relief train had come too late. Railroad cars were tossed around like toys according to one report. Rescue workers traveling south reported the first signs of hurricane wreckage at the Tavernier Railroad Station. (Sweeting—Byrum)

OCCUPANTS of this home *(above)* survived unharmed when hurricane wind picked it up from the foundations and lifted it 200 feet across the highway. The house was located between Tavernier and Snake Creek. (Sweeting)

WIND-DRIVEN WAVES pushed across Lower Matecumbe, destroying the ferry slip in the distance and washing out the railroad bed *(below)*. (Sweeting)

TREES the hurricane didn't uproot and wash away were left stripped. This was once a shady road on Islamorada *(left)*. (Sweeting)

IN THE HOT DAYS following the hurricane, bodies were recovered faster than they could be buried. On September 6, Florida Governor Dave Sholtz ordered the bodies cremated. National Guardsmen *(above)* prepare for a rifle salute to the dead. Across the washed out railroad bed, an American flag is unfurled. Black smoke of the cremation pyre *(right)* drifts across Snake Creek. Nineteen identified veterans and 19 unidentified civilians and veterans, all male, were cremated here September 7, 1935. (Sweeting)

WORK BEGAN on converting the railway into a highway on November 28, 1936. Above left the 14-foot width of the Seven-Mile Bridge, stretched out to 22 feet with I-beams which were given extra strength by rods welded into place at a 45 degree angle. A life preserver was hung over the end of the beam (above right) just in case the welder fell overboard. The Overseas Toll Bridge Commission, organized in 1933 to complete the missing links in the Overseas Highway, secured a $3.6 million federal grant in 1936. The commission paid $600,000 to the railroad for the right-of-way between Lower Matecumbe and Marathon, and gave a two year tax exemption to the railway for the rest of the bridges and right-of-way to Key West. The $3 million was earmarked to help convert the bridges and build the road. (Kerr)

A COMPLETED PORTION of the bridge curves over Pigeon Key as work continues toward the Moser Channel swing bridge. (Kerr)

A SPECIAL DETAIL had the job of catching fish to feed the hungry workmen. A good day's catch included four jewfish, including the monster in the center. One of the large work camps was located in Marathon. (Kerr)

LUTHER PINDER of Key West built this fishing camp and dining hall on a sandy beach on Boca Chica Key. The Boca Chica viaduct is in the background *(above)*. The wooden bridge *(below,* left center) leads to Stock Island in this 1937 photograph. Today this property is part of the U. S. Naval Air Station. (MDPL—Romer)

FERRIES were used to bridge the water gaps until the major bridges were converted. The Lower Matecumbe to Grassy Key ferry *(above)* was eliminated in the fall of 1937, but the Marathon to No Name Key ferry remained in operation until 1938 when the Seven-Mile and Bahia Honda Bridges were opened to automobile traffic. The ferry from Marathon arrives at No Name Key *(right)*. The ferry traveled the 15 miles in about two hours unless it got stuck. Looking from No Name Key to the ferry dock *(below)* where the *Pilgrim* (left) and *Key West* (right) are tied up. (MDPL—Romer)

FAYE MARIE PARKER *(left)* prepares to pull the string unveiling the monument to the 1935 hurricane victims on Upper Matecumbe Key. She was one of the Parkers who survived the hurricane by standing on an iron bed. The dedication *(below)* of the monument on November 14, 1937, attracted a huge crowd, including members of American Legion Posts and Auxiliaries from Dade and Monroe Counties. (Sweeting—Sandquist)

M. A. GOOD, an engineer with International Nickel Co., built a hurricane tower beside his oceanfront home on Plantation Key, a bastion of curved stones imported from England. Generators supplied power for his home and the tower. Natives considered him something of a recluse, but they believed he was wealthy because he paid for everything in cash. (Sprunt)

HAIL, HAIL, the gang's all here! Visiting Key Westers relax on this coconut studded island south of Little Torch Key. Newt and Ada Munson bought the island in the early 1920s. When he died he left Munson Island to his secretary, Ruth Ellison (third from right) who ran it as a fishing camp for a short time in the 1930s. Portions of the film *P. T. 109,* the World War II adventures of John F. Kennedy, were filmed here when it was owned by former state Senator John Spottswood. Spottswood sold the island in February 1972. (Bayly)

4 ★ SERVICE
★ Associated Press   ★ Wirephoto
★ International News Service
★ United Press

MIAMI DAILY NEWS

CITY EDITION

Weather—Partly cloudy tonight and Wednesday; possibly scattered showers. Details on page 4-A. Water temperature, 11 a. m., 78. Air temperature, 11 a. m., 78.

VOL. XLIII. NO. 108.   MIAMI, FLA., TUESDAY, MARCH 29, 1938   Three Sections   FIVE CENTS

HIGHWAY TO KEY WEST IS OPENED

—Daily News photo

KEY WEST LINKED TO MAINLAND AFTER THREE-YEAR LAPSE

Opening of the Overseas highway today linked Key West with the mainland for the first time since destruction of the Overseas railway by a storm on Labor day, 1935. Pictured tracks at the left give an idea of extent of the railway wreckage. Left inset is one of the ferries made obsolete by completion of the highway, a typical stretch of which is shown. Top right is one of the construction scenes. Lower right is an air view of Key West, with the barracks in the foreground. Bottom is one of the railroad bridges which has been converted for automobile traffic.

Celebration Marks Completion Of Link Spanning Last Gap

Daughter Of Cuban Consul Cuts Ribbon Letting Automobiles Make Island City Trip; Many Officials See Ceremony

By CECIL R. WARREN
(Daily News Staff Writer)

KEY WEST, March 29.—Key West today hung out its welcome signs and displayed the hospitality for which it is famous as neighboring Florida East Coast cities poured well-wishers into it in recognition of its again becoming connected with continental United States, this time by a broad overseas motor highway instead of the slender steel rails ripped up by the Labor day storm of 1935.

Impatient to do honor to visitors of neighboring cities hurrying to do honor to Key West, Monroe county and Key West officials, civic leaders and prominent citizens gathered at the home of Mayor of 5:40 a. m., formed a motorcade and set out to greet the well-wishers at Pigeon and Lower Matecumbe keys.

Symbolizing the conquering of the sea barrier, once surmounted by the pioneer, Henry M. Flagler, with his Florida East Coast Overseas railway, by the works progress administration forces, Senorita Ida Rodriguez, daughter of the Cuban consul in Key West, cut, at 9 a. m., at Pigeon key bridge, a slender ribbon barricade, while newsreel cameramen and newspaper photographers and writers recorded the event for posterity.

From there the party expected to go to Lower Matecumbe key for yet another program to be held at 2:30 p. m.

Station WIOD, through the facilities of its mobile transmitting unit, will broadcast, ceremonies in connection with the opening of the highway from 2 to 3 p. m. The broadcast will bring the remarks of county and Overseas highway commission officials and from a midway point on the highway will interview passengers in the first cars to traverse the new highway.

From Key West, Mayor Albury and William P. Porter, president of the First National bank, will speak and the Key West chorus will sing several dedication numbers.

In addition to hundreds of
(CONTINUED ON PAGE FOUR-A)

EUROPE FIGHTS TO KEEP CIVIL WAR IN SPAIN

New Threats Appear As Loyalists Battle With Backs To Wall

(By Associated Press)

LONDON, March 29.—Europe struggled today to keep Spain's civil war in Spain, against new threats it might spread.

The Spanish government, its back to the wall, accused Germany and Italy again of lending strong support to Generalissimo Francisco Franco's insurgent armies.

In Rome, the Fascist editor, Virginio Gayda, charged France and Russia were obstructing the withdrawal of foreign fighters from Spain, declaring Italy was ready to recall her forces when those countries did.

He warned that open French intervention in Spain would have "grave consequences" in the rest of Europe.

In London, the European non-intervention committee's sub-committee was summoned for Thursday. Great Britain then was expected to bring France into line with her plan to remove the foreign soldiers.

Insurgents, in a note to Britain, countered the government charges. They declared Barcelona authorities were planning an air raid on French soil with planes bearing Italian markings "to provoke an international conflict."

France's armies, with one foot planted in Catalonia province, waited for rest and reinforcements before launching what Insurgents hoped would be the death blow of the war. Catalonia is the heart of government Spain's resistance, its seat and industrial center.

Strengthened government lines from Franco's flanks and fortified hill-top trenches, long designed to save Catalonia from invasion, however, created the stiffest obstacles the Insurgents have faced in 30 days.

WITH THE INSURGENTS IN EASTERN SPAIN, March 29.—(P)— Generalissimo Franciseo Franco's troops advanced to within 12 miles of Lerida today and heard reports the government had started evacuation of the civilian population from that Catalonian stronghold.

The latest bitter phase of the Shantung campaign, nearly three months old, began yesterday. Fighting continued through the night. Chinese asserted the result was a victorious sweep northward, with the Japanese falling back.

Japanese disputed this, but the best available information indicated the Japanese had withdrawn from a gigantic hairpin area between the Tientsin-Pukow railway and the town of Lini.

In one of the several direct bat-
(CONTINUED ON PAGE FOUR-A)

WESTINGHOUSE HIT AT MART OPENING

Miami's Own hirligig
vs Behind The News

EOR—The Nazi atmosphere of Germany itself pervades the rman hydrographic vessel Meteor which put into Miami harbor yesterday. The visitors to the boat yesterday were greeted with the customary arm salute of the Brown Shirts. Below deck the pictures of Der Fuehrer Hitler are prominently displayed. The Nazi insignia, the swastika, embodied in the flag of the Third Reich, flies from the stern. Purpose of the hydrographic survey is to correct marine charts of the German admiralty, officers frankly admit.

GAMBLING — With Miami's gambling lid clamped down by executive order strenuous efforts are ding made to spring it for a final durge at "get away money." A gn, described as "influential," is t to be in Tallahassee trying onvince the governor the area s a few more days of "liberal" ilization. The gamblers, he id, are singing the blues and are urging the boss when they believed to convince everyone they "game." The answer is if they y during the height of the son, why would they wish son for the tail-end? Mean-Bill Hardie of the Miami association looks back on a announced his opposition to the al program in which his bill UED ON PAGE FOUR-A

OPICAL LATE SPECIAL
By JACK BELL
Daily News Sports Editor

'OPICAL PARK SCRATCHES FOR TODAY
'OND RACE—Bess B., Cautivo.
'ED RACE—Marbella, Cotoneaster, King Joy.
'TH RACE—Teddy Bean, Earl Porter.
'TH RACE—Payrack, Jildac Rose. Yenoc.

'ICAL PARK, March 29.—Today's featured offer-together six of the better grade routers in the at a mile and 60 yards, an allowance affair in '9 A. appears the likely winner. A clear track skies will prevail. Horses which seem to have

REORGANIZATION FIGHT TO HOUSE

Opponents Gird For Battle Against Approval Of Bill

(By Associated Press)

WASHINGTON, March 29.— Antiadministration Democrats joined house Republicans today in a final attempt to block enactment of the government reorganization bill, after a senate coalition had failed to prevent senate passage.

Roosevelt forces, jubilant over their 49-42 senate victory, declared house approval was only a matter of time.

Opponents, however, were fighting administration efforts to hasten the measure through a special reorganization committee and onto the house floor. Representative Taber (Rep., N. Y.), ranking minority committeeman, said he would demand public hearings on every phase of the bill.

Senator Clark (Dem., Mo.) and other foes said they believed the telegrap ic campaign against the Seagraott, first cousin of Henry, said here today. He is in Miami on business.

Mrs. Seagraott was vacationing in Florida for several weeks, spending several days with Mr. and Mrs. Herbert Seagraott in Cocoa. She sailed aboard the Shawnee at Miami March 22. She was reportedly in good spirits when she embarked.

Hungary Next For Hitler?

(By Associated Press)

KNOXVILLE, March 29.— William R. Dodd, former U. S. ambassador to Germany, told an audience here last night that Hungary and not Czechoslovakia was the next objective of Adolf Hitler's Nazi organization. Hitler, he said, already has ordered construction of warships on the Danube and these will menace Hungary, Rumania and Bulgaria.

MIAMI VISITOR LOST FROM SHIP AT SEA

Mrs. Henry Seagroatt Missing When Shawnee Docks

Mrs. Henry J. Seagroatt, 55, of Berlin, N. Y., disappeared from the Clyde-Mallory liner vessel SS. Shawnee on its latest trip from Miami to New York, Herbert Seagroatt of Cocoa reported here today.

The missing passenger was last seen aboard the vessel at 8:15 a. m. Friday, March 25. The craft docked in New York at 2 p. m. Friday. Mrs. Seagroatt's husband, a wholesale florist in Berlin, met the boat but could not find his wife aboard.

Telegraphic advices indicate Mrs. Seagroatt was lost at sea. Herbert Seagroatt, first cousin of Henry, said here today.

RECALL LISTS GROW STEADILY

Canvass In Southwest Section Adds 1,000 Names To Petitions

More than 1,000 additional names were obtained on petitions seeking recall of Mayor Robert R. Williams and Commissioners John W. DuBose and Ralph B. Ferguson as workers began a systematic canvass of the Progressive Government association.

The workers, for the first time during the campaign in the southwest section, worked only above the city's Second and Third sts, Tryon said, and additional help was put on today to aid in the canvassing there. Workers now are being paid on the basis of $1 a day and a commission for each name obtained.

Tryon said he planned to consult with an attorney today on advisability of arresting R. A. Fletcher, former office manager for Welfare Director Louis K. MacReynolds, on charges growing out of the theft of a petition blank from a woman worker. Leniency in Fletcher's case, the committee chairman said, apparently had prompted other attempts of enemies of the movement to obtain petitions.

The recall committee today ordered 150 additional petition blanks from the city clerk, making a total of 450 which will be in circulation when these are delivered tomorrow, or sufficient room for 45,000 signers. Tryon said the committee hoped to have 12,000 signatures by the end of this week.

Just Love, Swain Says

(By International News Service)

NEW YORK, March 29.— "It's spring and I love her," explained Hyman Seidorf, 20, today as police asked him why he had smacked Miss Ida Sherman, 17 in the eye. Hyman was sent to Bellevue hospital for mental observation.

HARBOR PARLEY SET AT COLUMBUS HOTEL

City And Federal Officials To Discuss Development

Members of the federal maritime commission will meet with local shipping interests at 10 a. m. tomorrow at the Columbus hotel to discuss the possibilities and future of Miami's harbor.

Among those who will represent the city and Propeller club of Miami will be Charles E. Albury, shipping agent; George Schelbenberger, Boatswain Thomas E. Grady, rate and traffic consultant and others.

The maritime commission is seeking first hand information on Miami and other harbors.

APRIL 1 DEADLINE ON TAX EXEMPTION

The office of J. N. Lummus, Jr. county tax assessor, today was crowded with scores of persons anxious to file their homestead exemption applications before the expiration date, April 1. Already more than 16,000 such requests have been made, showing a substantial increase over preceding years. Intangible personal property tax returns also should be filed before April 1.

CHINESE ROUT BIG JAP ARMY

Nipponese Reported Retreating On 100-Mile Battle Front

(By Associated Press)

SHANGHAI, March 29.—A great Chinese army today was reported to be pushing back Japanese along a 100-mile front in bitter battle for Central China.

On the battle, along a furiously-contested line in Southern Shantung province stretching eastward from the Tientsin-Pukow railway, observers believed the fate of Central China depended.

More than 100,000 men were engaged on each side. Each army reported extremely heavy casualties for the enemy.

MEXICO UNABLE TO PEDDLE OIL

Lack Of Foreign Markets Brings Urgent Problem To Government

MEXICO CITY, March 29.—The lack of foreign markets pressed urgent problems today upon the Mexican government's newly acquired oil industry.

There have been 11 days without sales abroad since the government took over 17 American and British oil companies on March 18, and the nation's oil tanks are filled near to capacity.

Production has been curtailed 45 to 75 per cent, but even so it appears there soon will be no place to house the "black gold."

The problem of storage space is specifically involved, but the broader aspects embrace economic adjustment.

The suspension of purchases of Mexican silver by the United States Treasury started the pen on a rapid decline. Mexicans believe a further suspension as retaliation for expropriation of the $400,000,000 foreign-owned oil industry.

Some fear the United States now is considering also an upward adjustment on tariffs on Mexican goods—this fear based on Secretary Morgenthau's statement Sunday the United States intended to review commercial and financial relationships with Mexico.

Declining business sales were noted here. One leading department
(CONTINUED ON PAGE FOUR-A)

Spanish War Virtually Over, Noted Correspondent Thinks

Barcelona To Fall In Two Or Three Weeks, Knickerbocker Says

(EDITOR'S NOTE: Spain's civil war is "virtually over" with the insurgents victorious and Barcelona fating captive within two or three weeks, in the opinion today of H. R. Knickerbocker, famous foreign correspondent, who spent many months watching the fighting in Spain.)

By H. R. KNICKERBOCKER
(International News Service Staff Correspondent)
(Copyright, 1938)

PARIS, March 29.—The Spanish war is virtually over.

Insurgent Generalissimo Francisco Franco has won, and the loyalist government today would capitulate were it not for communist pressure.

It will take Franco two or three weeks to capture Barcelona in the
(CONTINUED ON PAGE FOUR-A)

CELEBRATION of the completed Overseas Highway was delayed until the big Fourth of July weekend of 1938. Miss Bernice Brantley, "Miss Key West" prepares to snip the ribbon dedicating the Bahia Honda Bridge July 2, 1938. Key West Mayor Willard M. Albury stands beside Miss Brantley as the ceremony is broadcast over Miami radio station WIOD. (Papy—Roberts)

BUSINESS CENTER of Tavernier in June, 1938. H. S. McKenzie built the large building (center) for a theater, but after the hurricane it became the Tavernier Hotel. Next door is the service station and Tavern Store. The old county road has since become the northbound lane of U. S. 1. (MDPL—Romer)

LOOKING SOUTHWESTERLY down old Highway 905 on Key Largo. The area shown is in the vicinity of today's Horne's Restaurant. Only a few homes dotted the highway in 1938. (MDPL—Romer)

GREEN TURTLES are beached on the Florida Keys. Exact location was not identified by the photographer, but it is believed to be in the Upper Keys. (MDPL—Romer)

L. E. GOETZ built this house of native coral on what was then called Jewfish Key in the late 20's. The Key was renamed Greyhound Key and in more recent years, Fiesta Key. A laundry gas tank explosion some 20 years ago set the interior on fire and the stone building was gutted. (MDPL—Romer)

"STOP! EAT SEAFOOD," the sign invites motorists to the original Green Turtle Inn on Islamorada. The same building is in use today. Building with light-colored roof down the road is one of the poured concrete homes built after the 1935 hurricane. (MDPL—Romer)

ISLAMORADA settlement and Post Office on June 21, 1938. The Post Office was located on the site of today's Islamorada Post Office. (MDPL—Romer)

MOTORISTS had a free ride down the highway until they got to Lower Matecumbe. Here an attendent collected $1 per vehicle and 25 cents for each passenger. Tolls were used to pay off the indebtedness of the Overseas Road and Toll Bridge District. In the background is the Toll Gate Inn. (MDPL—Romer)

CRAIG was a community located between Lower Matecumbe and Long Key. R. W. Craig displays a reminder of the killer '35 hurricane—a coconut with a timber driven through it *(left)*. Across the highway from his store, Craig sold gas at this open air shed. This was the first gas stop after passing the toll gate. (MDPL—Romer)

THE FEW RESIDENTS of Craig and visitors who tied up boats in the rear for fuel enjoyed this "swimming hole." Craig called it "shark and barracuda-proof." (MDPL—Romer)

BONEFISH KEY on the northeasterly tip of Grassy Key was another motorist haven for gas and food. It was near where Bonefish Harbor Marina is now. (MDPL—Romer)

MOTORISTS could eat and spend the night at Hall's Restaurant and Cabins. The taller building is the Marathon Sundry Store. The highway which opened in 1932 passed in front of the building. Motorists would drive down to the lower end of Marathon to catch the ferry to No Name Key. (MDPL—Romer)

CAPTAIN HARRY SNOW, SR. gained a reputation as a crack bonefish guide in Marathon. He shows off one of the "grey ghosts of the flats." (Snow)

A LARGE SIGN proudly proclaims the Marathon Yacht Basin. It was located on the bayside of Marathon and was also known as Thompson's Yacht Basin. (MDPL—Romer)

THE SEVEN-MILE BRIDGE at Pigeon Key curves toward Moser Channel. Later a ramp was built from the bridge to the Key, and it became the headquarters of the toll district operations. (MDPL—Romer)

THE BIG PINE KEY INN, a well-known stopover during railroad days. This 1938 photograph was taken after the old railroad bed in front of the Inn was converted into a highway. (MDPL—Romer)

PRESIDENT FRANKLIN D. ROOSEVELT traveled down the Overseas Highway from Miami to Key West, February 19, 1939. Accompanied by Monroe and Dade County officials, the President stopped here on West Summerland Key to inspect a Conservation Corps Camp. Left to right are: a Mr. Smith; Miami attorney Paul H. Marks; John Slade, chairman of the Overseas Road and Toll Bridge Commission; Key West Mayor Willard M. Albury; Bridge Commissioner John H. Costar, Sr.; Miami Mayor Alex Orr; Monroe County Commissioner C. C. Symonette; and former Miami Mayor Ed Sewell. (MCC)

102

KNOWN AS the new cut-over, this road was constructed so motorists then using the No Name Key ferry could cut across Big Pine Key to the highway being constructed along the railroad right of way. It is commonly called Prison Farm Road today. (MDPL—Romer)

FISHERMAN prepares to take on ice before leaving Pedro's Dock in Tavernier in November, 1937. The dock and fish house were located behind what is now Lindsley Lumber. (LC—Rothstein)

"HARRY HIMSELF"—Harry Harris when he operated the Tavernier Cafe beside the hotel. A Hershey Bar was only five cents then. (Harris)

HARRY HARRIS (left) sits down to enjoy a beer with a customer, Carol Bishop. The older man at the end of the bar is John Staff. The bartender is Bob Bratton; Donnie Donaldson is on the far right. Waitress and man with back to camera are not identified. Harris later converted the cafe into his office. He has served as a county commissioner for 28 years and is currently Mayor of Monroe County. (Harris)

WATER FOR SALE! At four cents a gallon, that added up to $40 per 1000 back in 1939. Charley Toppino (far right) sold water hauled from Homestead to Marathon. Also in the photograph (from left) are Frank Toppino, William Gibson, and three friends. (Toppino)

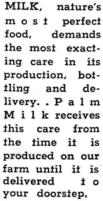
THE PARKS started their dairy on Stock Island in 1934. In the late 1930s, they bought out the cows of the Convent of Mary Immaculate when the nuns decided to get rid of them. They often had as many as 40 cows to supply the milk. The dairy closed at the onset of World War II. Milk was delivered in Key West with this truck (below), and at left is an advertisement for "bottled health," the grade A pasteurized milk supplied by Palm Dairy. (Park)

TOMMY CASH heads away from Stock Island to Raccoon Key (now known as Key Haven) in his sailing skiff (above). Cash lived on Stock Island where he earned a living making charcoal and fishing. He also helped out Alton ("Ikey") and Helen Park who operated the Palm Dairy. The Park's children, Joyce (Perez) and Robert are going sailing with Cash. (Park)

The Florida Keys since 1940

THE NATIONAL AUDUBON SOCIETY established a research laboratory on Bottlepoint Key, north of Tavernier, to study the nesting roseate spoonbill in April, 1940. Robert P. Allen, the society's director of sanctuaries, lived on the Key. His studies were published in 1942. (Sprunt)

ROSEATE SPOONBILLS fly majestically over the Keys. The National Audubon Society's work helped protect this disappearing bird. (Sprunt)

IVORY, COPPER PANS, and slave irons were recovered from a sunken ship off Marathon in the early 1940s. The artifacts are examined by Haley Hamlin, Art McKee, Charlie Slater, Mrs. Jane H. Crile, and Dr. George Crile, Jr. (McKee)

KAY AND JACK Wilkinson were still living in a tent home in the early 40's. They described this as a "typical Sunday gathering." (Wilkinson)

ROUGHING IT on the Keys in 1941, Jack Wilkinson (center) and his friend enjoy an outdoor shave at Planter. Jack's son watches the lather fly. (Wilkinson)

JACK WILKINSON continued to make a living by catching fish and turtle, and by selling aquatic specimens to the Marine Studios at St. Augustine. At right, he poses with son Johnny beside a jewfish. (Wilkinson)

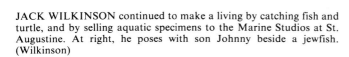

WILKINSON sold turtles to Marineland. He kept them in water pens commonly called crawls, or kraals. Here a recently netted turtle is dropped into the pen. (Wilkinson)

THE SIGN at left identifies Wilkinson home as a collecting base for specimens bound for Marineland at St. Augustine. (Wilkinson)

LITTLE JOHNNY WILKINSON is dwarfed by this sea monster—a manta ray. Before the manta was boated, a shark took three big mouthfuls from the body. (Wilkinson)

108

FRIGATE birds or man-o'-war birds appear awkward while perching among mangroves on Marquesas Key. In flight, the birds float on graceful wings which sometimes span eight feet. Despite its size, the man-o'-war can swoop down from great heights on a surface fish and without wetting a feather pluck it from the sea. (Sprunt)

THE FREIGHTER *S. S. Benwood*, loaded with phosphate, collided with the tanker, *Robert C. Tuttle*, during the night of April 9, 1942 off Key Largo. One man was killed and the heavily damaged *Benwood* went aground in what is now John Pennekamp State Park. Some reports indicated the *Benwood* was shelled by a German U-boat, but offical records show no U-boats in the area on that date. (McKee)

THE AGE-OLD WATER PROBLEM of the Florida Keys was solved in a unique arrangement. The Navy and Florida Keys Aqueduct Commission signed an agreement in March, 1941 to build a 130 mile pipeline from the Florida City well-fields to Key West. A Navy officer surveys the 18-inch diameter pipe at Florida City *(above)*, while perched on the end of the pipe, a supervisor *(left)* watches workmen float the line into place for the underwater crossing at Tavernier Creek. *Below:* Pipe is unloaded and laid alongside the highway in the Upper Keys. While the pipeline was being laid, three wells were being dug at Florida City. (U. S. Navy)

THE CONTRACTOR, William Bros. Corp., who started laying pipe on November 28, 1941, was under pressure to complete the pipeline because of the military personnel overflowing Key West during World War II. A ditcher straddles a trench where the pipeline will be buried. (U. S. Navy)

HARD-HAT DIVER Art McKee "suits up" to go beneath the Moser Channel swingbridge to secure the pipeline in 1942. In this dive to 22 feet, McKee was almost drowned when a pin came out of his helmet. Manuel Asura, McKee's tender on the dive, sensed something had happened and managed to pull McKee to safety. (McKee)

WORKMEN remove a temporary walkway used during the pipeline installation on Bahia Honda Bridge. The contractor finally had his job accepted October 18, 1944, and was paid a total of $1,719,017. (U. S. Navy)

A RIFLE RANGE was set up on Stock Island during World War II. It was located near the present day site of Florida Keys Community College. (Allen)

BECAUSE OF the vulnerability of the Navy's lifeline—the Overseas Highway—bridges were checked out routinely against possible sabotage during the war years. The intelligence office in Key West received many reports of spies—including one from an elderly lady who called to say, "I have just completed a list of 100 genuine spies—please come over at once." (Allen)

U. S. COAST GUARD training camp at Marathon during World War II. Guardsmen were put through "boot camp" here. An airport was also built in Marathon as a practice landing field. (Allen)

MONROE COUNTY originally acquired property on Boca Chica Key for a muncipal airport, but with the outbreak of the war, the Army took it over and built three paved runways. However, the Navy wanted Boca Chica to train pilots for carriers, and in April, 1943, the Army was shoved out. Old Highway 4-A is at top of photgraph; new highway is at right. (U. S. Navy)

AFTER THE NAVY TOOK over Boca Chica, the expanded facility included 56 barracks, eight bachelor officer quarters, a theater, a recreation area, three hangars, and pilot training facilities. It hit a peak of 4,-000 personnel in early 1945. (U. S. Navy)

A HURRICANE in mid-October 1944 easily tore apart this prefabricated office building at Boca Chica Naval Air Station. (U. S. Navy)

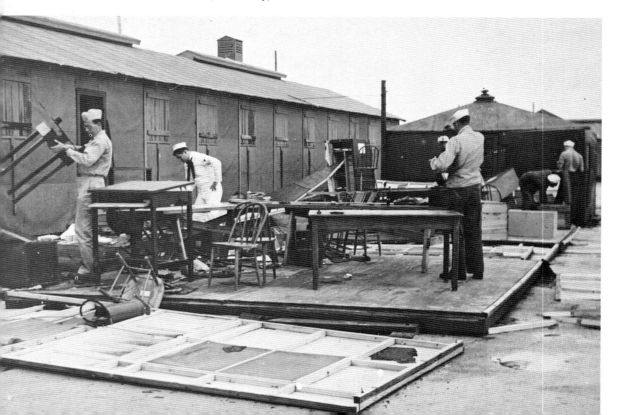

THE TAVERN STORE, a landmark in the Upper Keys, was relocated across U. S. 1 in a new store in 1944. This building is still in use under the same name. (Byrum)

"I DEDICATE this road to the greatness of the Keys," Florida Governor Spessard L. Holland remarked on May 16, 1944. It was the opening of a "new" Overseas Highway, and his wife prepared to snip the ribbon atop the Bahia Honda Bridge. Old wooden bridges were replaced with concrete spans, the highway was straightened, and 18 miles clipped off the Old 4-A scenic route along the Atlantic Ocean. Tolls were lifted April 15, 1954. (Papy—Roberts)

ELIZABETH McIVER operated a chic cruisewear shop in Marathon. She sold out in 1951 and the building today is the office of Carter and Son.

ALMA AND HER SNAKES

ALMA CAGLE BISHOP had her gift shop of reptile bags, wallets, and belts located in the Flamingo Bar. She also kept a few live snakes. Many a heavy drinker must have thought he was in a snake pit when Alma and her pets came by the bar. (Rondeau)

116

GILL AND MAUD Spence had one of Marathon's most popular watering holes—the Flamingo Bar. Maud is seated at right. (Rondeau)

BEHIND THE BAR of the Flamingo Cocktail Lounge, Maud Spence (right) lifts a "Melrose Ginny"—a drink said to have had quite a punch. (Rondeau)

117

SILVER BULLION bars recovered from a galleon wrecked on the reef off Key Largo brought the rough, hard-working McKee money and fame (*above right*). McKee shows off a bar which he sold to the Smithsonian Institution in Washington, D.C. (*above left*). His rich finds also included this gold quarter-doubloon and the larger silver piece-of-eight (*right*) which were unearthed from the ocean (*below*). (McKee)

ART McKEE, the pioneer treasure hunter of the Keys, had salvaged enough material from Spanish wrecks to open his own Museum of Sunken Treasure *(above)* in 1949 on Plantation Key. A hard-helmet diver who worked as a commercial salvor based in Homestead, McKee got hooked on treasure salvage work after recovering cannon off the Upper Keys. What appears as a clump of coral *(right)* is conglomerate from a wreck that, when X-rayed, reveals a variety of coins and artifacts *(below)*. (McKee)

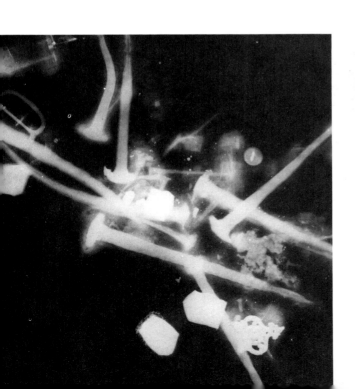

119

BUTTONS jumps for a fish held by Dotty Albury. The 13-foot jump by the dolphin was part of the act at Theater of the Sea at Windley Key. (Albury)

A PUMPING STATION was built in Marathon to maintain pressure and push more water down the Navy pipeline to Key West where the demand for water had increased. Charley Toppino and Sons, Inc. completed the booster station by mid-1946. (U.S. Navy)

THIS ROAD SIGN alerted motorists that Key Vaca was coming up. Marathon was still called Key Vaca in the late 1940s—a name dating back to the 18th Century. (FSU)

120

THIS WAS an early dredge-and-fill project in Marathon. After the war ended, "Navy water" could be diverted for civilian usage and this spurred development. The filled land in the foreground was for a mobile home subdivision. (Parrish)

FOURTH OF JULY and a big parade! McIver's Tropical Togs of Marathon sponsored this float in 1949. Those in the photograph (from left) are: Marion Parrish, Pat Ziggenhagen Mercier, Elizabeth McIver, Alma Cagle Bishop, and Betty Parkhurst Rondeau. The youngster is Allan Parrish, son of Mrs. Parrish. (McIver)

WHITEY AND DIANA WHITE operated the Marathon Sundry Store (*below*) when this photograph was taken in the late 1940s. (Anderson)

GRANTLAND RICE'S cameramen are caught by the candid camera against the backdrop of Bahia Honda Bridge. They were making a movie on the Florida Keys in 1949. (FSU)

TAVERNIER was beginning to show signs of development in the late 40's with homes and businesses going up along U.S. 1. In the center of the photograph is the Tavern Store with a Miami-bound Greyhound bus out front. (Byrum)

THE SUNSET TEA ROOM on Key Largo advertised itself as the home of native Key lime pie. (FSU)

"YE OLE FESHIN HOLE" in Marathon attracted anglers needing bait and tackle, and for many years was a landmark for the motorist traveling U.S. 1. In the late 1940s a motion picture theater was located next door. Capt. Johnny and Wilma Brantner, who operated the Feshin Hole, would leave cans of gasoline outside the store at night for motorists to purchase on an honor system. (Anderson)

MARATHON FISHING GUIDE Harry M. Snow, Sr. (standing) watches Mrs. Grace H. Tauck hook a bonefish. In early 1950, she caught a 12 pound, 14.5 ounce bonefish that was an American record and the Women's World Record. (Snow)

KEY COLONY BEACH as it appeared in the early 1950s. Developer Phil Sadowski had a causeway built from U.S. 1 to the water's edge where he created what was to become the city of Key Colony Beach. (Anderson)

JACK WATSON mans the air hose as Robert W. Hines, artist with the U.S. Fish and Wildlife Service, prepares for an exploratory dive into the small freshwater lake known as "Blue Hole" on Big Pine Key. (Watson)

FEWER THAN 50 of the tiny Key deer could be accounted for in 1949 when conservationists rallied to save this species that is unique to the Florida Keys. This buck *(center)* is only 27-inches high at the shoulder. His habitat reduced to a few keys around Big Pine Key, the Key deer's plight generated a national compaign that resulted in Congress establishing the National Key Deer Refuge in August 1957. Jack Watson, a federal bird-refuge manager in the Keys, became the first full-time protector and overseer of the Key deer in the early 1950s *(bottom)*. Before setting out on a survey of the Key deer habitat, Watson chats with two men from the U. S. Fish and Wildlife Service in front of the Big Pine Key Inn. *(above)*. For his personal dedication in protecting the endangered Key deer, Watson was chosen Conservationist of the Year (1973) by the National Wildlife Federation. (Watson)

126

"GIVE 'EM HELL" Harry S. Truman and "The King of the Keys," Monroe County's State Rep. Bernie C. Papy Sr., smile and greet each other with that firm politician's handshake. The President met local officials at Boca Chica Naval Air Station before zipping off to "The Little White House" on the U.S. Naval Station in Key West. Standing between Truman and Papy is Key West Mayor C. B. Harvey and an unidentified Boy Scout. The photograph was take in the early 1950s. (Papy-Brodhead)

ONE OF THE FIRST projects of the newly created Monroe County Mosquito District was to cover the city of Key West's dump on Stock Island. Bulldozer operator Sonny Hinde works here covering the mosquito breeding ground in the early 1950s.

TENTACLES OF DEVELOPMENT stretch from booming Marathon into offshore waters. Taken in 1950, this aerial view looks toward Miami. (Rondeau)

128